Impact
ISSUES

30 KEY ISSUES TO HELP YOU EXPRESS YOURSELF IN ENGLISH

Richard R. Day
Junko Yamanaka

 LONGMAN

Published by
Pearson Education Asia Pte Ltd
317 Alexandra Road
#04-01 Alexandra Building
Singapore 159965

and Associated Companies throughout the world.

This book was developed for Addison Wesley Longman Asia ELT by Lateral Communications Limited.

First published 1998
Reprinted 1999 (three times)

Produced by Addison Wesley Longman China Ltd, Hong Kong
SWTC/05

Project director: Michael Rost
Development editor: Anne McGannon
Project coordinator: Keiko Kimura
Production coordinator: Eric Yau
Text design: Keiko Kimura, Lori Margulies
Cover design: Lori Margulies
Illustrations: Mark Ziemann
Recording supervisor: David Joslyn
Photographs: Diamar Portfolios, Ken Kitamura, Keiko Kimura, Photo Disc, Rubberball Productions

ISBN Textbook and Audio CD 962 00 1480 4

ACKNOWLEGEMENTS

The authors and editors wish to thank the teachers and students who contributed to this project through interviews, review and piloting reports.

In particular, we wish to thank:

Mikyung Chang	Jun Yokoi	Paul Kennedy
Susan Gilfert	Kenny Harsch	Greg Sanders
Greg Goodmacher	Sook Kyoung Kim	Karen Kinoshita
Naoko Ozeki	Donna Prather	Atsuoko Kurawaki

We wish to express special thanks to the teachers at Trident School of Languages, especially:

Michael Cholewinski	Kuriko Mizuno	Naomi Yamada
Rika Majima	Tomoko Sato	Eiko Yazawa
Ryoko Mizoguchi	Yoshiko Shimoto	

We express our appreciation to the teachers who completed the initial surveys about the teaching of reading, discussion and global education that informed the topics in this book:

Paul Arenson	Marianne Jarvis	David Loyd
Patricia Callaghan	Raymond Keenan	Richard Marshall
Julian Dobson	Barbara Kerr	Laura Swanson
Marc Goozee	Yukio Kimura	Lorraine Koch Yao
David Holden		

We would also like to thank the Pearson Education staff for their support and their valuable advice throughout the development of the project.

From the authors, special thanks go to Mike Rost and Anne McGannon for their extraordinary work and dedication to the project.

HOW TO USE

Impact ISSUES

TO THE STUDENT

You can use this book by yourself or in class with other students. Here are some ideas to help you when you use it by yourself:

1   Look at the TABLE OF CONTENTS. What topics do you like? Choose a topic that you really like.

2   Go to the topic and read the story. Read as quickly as you can, but don't go too fast. Try to understand the story; don't worry if you don't know all the words. And don't stop to look up words in your dictionary! You can look up words that you don't know in the GLOSSARY *after* you have finished reading.

3   Then listen to the story on the CD. Read along silently as you listen. It is a good idea to do this activity two or three times, because it helps you understand spoken English. It also helps you with the pronunciation of words you don't know.

4   Next, read the WHAT DO YOU THINK? opinions. Choose the opinions you agree with.

5   Then read the instructions for LOOKING AT THE ISSUE. Complete the table with your ideas.

6   Finally, study the INTERACTION TIP in the back of the book . When you speak English in the classroom or with someone outside school, try to use the tips you have learned.

It is not necessary to start with the first topic and work to the end of the book. You can try any topic you wish. Choose the topics that interest you most.

If you have a friend who wants to speak English, try using this book together. It's fun to compare your ideas with another person.

TO THE TEACHER

Impact Issues is a collection of 30 current topics that young adult students have expressed an interest in discussing. The topics are organized into five "Issues," and each topic is carefully presented with exercises to help students understand the issues and express their own opinions.

There are many ways you can use the material in this book to help your students improve their reading, listening and speaking abilities in English. Here is one possible procedure:

1   Begin by looking over the Table of Contents. Choose the Issues and the Topics that will be of greatest interest to your students. You don't have to start with the first issue.

2   In class, have the students read the Introduction questions to start thinking about the topic before they read.

3   Next, have the students turn to the Topic and read the story. Tell them to read quickly, and advise them not to look up words in their dictionaries. They should focus on the parts in bold type, as these are the main ideas of the reading. When they have finished reading, you can give them a couple of minutes to find words they don't know in the Glossary.

4   If you have a CD player, you can play the CD and have the students read along silently as they listen. This is an important activity because it helps the students understand the rhythm, stress and intonation of spoken English, as well as the pronunciation of unfamiliar words.

5   Now have the students read the What Do You Think? opinions. The purpose of this activity is to get the students to think about different opinions or viewpoints on the topic. The opinions are not numbered or ordered logically, to encourage the students to select the opinions they like or agree with.

6   The students then compare the opinion(s) they have chosen with a partner or in a small group. They can either read the ones they have chosen, or try to give the opinions in their own words. There are no right or wrong answers to this activity. The students can consult the Interaction Tips in the back of the book for simple conversation patterns to use when they exchange opinions.

7   Finally, have the students try the Looking at the Issue activity. The goal of this activity is to help the students think critically about some aspect of the topic. You can have the students do this activity alone, in pairs or in small groups. If the students work alone, have them share their ideas with their classmates, either in pairs or in small groups, when they are finished. Again, there are no right or wrong answers to this activity.

This entire procedure can take from 30 to 60 minutes, depending on the English ability of your students and how long you want to spend on each activity.

OPTION:

In the back of the book, there are 30 Interaction Tips. These tips present basic vocabulary and grammatical structures to help the students exchange ideas. You can present one Interaction Tip for each topic and demonstrate it with the students. Then you can have them practice in pairs. Remind the students to use the tips when discussing their opinions with their classmates.

Once the students have finished a topic, you can try a follow-up activity:
• a written assignment on the topic that asks the students to express their opinion, summarize and analyze the story or tell a similar story of their own
• a presentation for which the students find similar, current articles to share with the class
• a debate in which the students formally prepare, present and discuss their ideas on the topic

We hope that you and your students will enjoy using this book. We hope that your students' interest and motivation will increase, and that their reading, thinking and discussion ability in English will develop. Please write us with your comments and suggestions. We would love to hear from you.

CONTENTS

If you are using the *Impact* Coursebooks, try these units in *Impact Issues:*

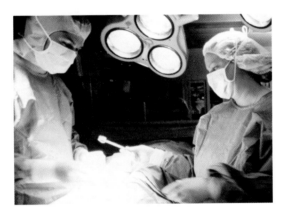

SSUES IN LIFESTYLES

- Do you like eating meat?
- Do you think humans need to eat meat?
- A professor of food science gives her views on the topic.

3 WHAT'S FOR DINNER?

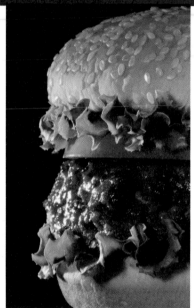

1 WHY LEARN ENGLISH?

- Is learning English necessary?
- Is it a waste of time?
- A university student gives his opinion.

2 FOREVER SINGLE

- What do you think about marriage?
- Is marriage a good idea for everyone?
- A young professional woman gives her opinion about marriage and freedom.

4
LAST CHANCE

- Are we treating the earth well?

- Are our lifestyles dangerous to the environment?

- A time traveler from the year 2500 returns to earth with a warning.

- What are the problems of having too many cars?

- Can anything be done about these problems?

- One Asian city provides a possible solution.

6
TRAFFIC JAM

5
TAKE THE MONEY AND RUN

Do professional athletes play only for money?

- Is money more important than everything else?

- A sports star has to make a difficult decision.

Why Learn **English?**

1

Jin Lee has studied English for a long time. Read the story and find out: How does he feel about learning English?

I am a fourth-year student at a good university in Korea. I will graduate in four months and take a job with a company in a small town near Seoul. I have spent almost 10 years learning English. And let me tell you, **it has been a waste of time.**

To begin with, **I will probably never use English in my work**. My job will be with a taxi company. Everyone speaks Korean. The owner of the company is Korean and all of the employees are Korean, too. The taxi drivers themselves do not need to speak English because there are very few foreign visitors in our small town.

I don't need English in my free time, either. If I want to read about what is happening in foreign countries, **I can read Korean newspapers and magazines. I can learn all about other countries by reading in my native language, not English.**

And of course all the television stations carry international stories, so **I don't have to watch the news in English in order to understand what is happening all over the world.**

I think of the many hours, days, weeks, even years that I spent in school and at home studying English. **Just think of what else I could have studied instead of English**. I could have studied more history, so that I could understand my country better. Or I could have read more literature, to help me understand the great writers of my country.

Instead, I spent so much time studying English. **And for what reason?** So I could pass examinations? What a terrible waste of time. I really can't understand why people need to study English for so many years.

IN THE GLOSSARY (PAGE 90)
• *a waste of time* • *to begin with* • *employees* • *literature*

WHAT DO YOU THINK?

Which opinions do you agree with?
Check as many as you want.

❑ English is the most important international language. We should all study it until we're good at it, even if it takes several years.

❑ If you need English for work or travel, you should learn it. But not everybody needs to learn it—for a lot of people, it's just a waste of time and energy.

❑ You may think you don't need English now, but who knows? You might need it in the future. So, it's better to be prepared.

❑ I think learning a foreign language is very important. But it doesn't have to be English. Other languages are important, too, especially the languages of neighboring countries.

❑ We should study English but not for so long. The people who really need it can continue to study it if they want.

Now exchange your ideas with a classmate.

TURN TO PAGE 80 FOR AN INTERACTION TIP.

LOOKING AT THE ISSUE

Here are some reasons for learning English.
Can you think of an argument against each reason?

For

If you know English, you can travel anywhere.

You can watch American movies.

English is the language for computers.

You can get a good job.

You can have international friends.

your idea:

Against

Not really. There are many places where English is not used.

*F*OREVER SINGLE

2

Hope Hamilton doesn't want to get married.
Read this story and find out why.

Hope Hamilton should be excited. Her boyfriend, Bob, asked her to marry him. But after thinking about it very carefully, **Hope has decided she does not want to get married.**

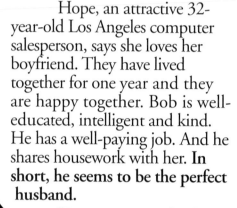

Hope, an attractive 32-year-old Los Angeles computer salesperson, says she loves her boyfriend. They have lived together for one year and they are happy together. Bob is well-educated, intelligent and kind. He has a well-paying job. And he shares housework with her. **In short, he seems to be the perfect husband.**

"But marriage is for fools and dreamers," says Hope. "I mean, who in their right mind would willingly give up their freedom for another person?"

Marriage changes people, Hope believes. Husbands and wives begin to take each other for granted. Bob helps with the shopping and cooking now, but Hope thinks that this might change if they get married. She might have to do much more of the traditional woman's work—cooking, shopping and housework.

If she gets married, **Hope believes that she will change, too.** She says she is very different from when she was 22 years old, and will be a different person in

10 more years. So she wonders if she can remain happy with Bob.

Hope simply feels that marriage is not the best relationship. "Hey, **almost half of all marriages end in divorce.** And many people who do stay married may not be happy. I have a lot of married friends whose marriages are not very good."

Hope also thinks that marriage will die out in the next century. "So many people all over the world live together now without being married. There is really no need for marriage to continue," she believes.

"Don't get me wrong," Hope explains, "I am not a crazy person who wants to live a life separated from other people, especially men. I love people, and that's another reason why marriage is not the best relationship. There are too many cool people in the world. **I do not want to be tied to just one person all of my life. I enjoy being free.**"

IN THE GLOSSARY (PAGE 90)
• **attractive** • **well-educated** • **willingly** • **take each other for granted** • **separated**

WHAT DO YOU THINK?

What do you think about marriage?
Check the opinions you agree with.

❏ I don't like marriage because it means "giving up freedom."

❏ Maybe marriage is not a good idea. It's difficult to live happily with one person all your life. People change.

❏ Marriage is important. It keeps society together. It's really necessary.

❏ When you meet the right person, you'll want to get married. It's natural.

❏ If you want to have children, marriage is important. Children need a stable home.

Now exchange your ideas with a classmate.

TURN TO PAGE 80 FOR AN INTERACTION TIP.

LOOKING AT THE ISSUE

Should a person stay single or get married?
What are some good reasons for each one?

Staying single is good because...

Getting married is good because...

Many marriages end in divorce anyway.

If you meet the right person, you will live happily together.

When you get married, you have to give up your freedom.

Marriages keep society together.

People change. You can't love one person forever.

It's important to bring up children with a mother and father.

your idea:

What's for Dinner?

Dr. Heidi Cornfield, a professor of food science, is being interviewed about her new book, What's for Dinner? Read the interview and find out: What does she think is wrong with the American diet?

Interviewer: You have some very strong ideas about what Americans eat, Professor Cornfield. Could you tell our audience about some of them?

Cornfield: I'd be delighted. First, **I think that Americans eat too much meat.** We can get protein from other types of food, not just meat. For example, tofu is rich in protein. We really don't need to eat meat to live.

Interviewer: Maybe, but some of our listeners really like nice thick juicy hamburgers. They might not need them, but they sure like them.

Cornfield: I agree with you. **But there are health reasons to stop eating meat.**

Interviewer: What do you mean, Professor?

Cornfield: **Eating meat, especially beef, can cause heart disease.** Thousands of Americans die from heart disease every year.

Interviewer: That's interesting. Are there other reasons why we should stop eating meat?

Cornfield: Yes. **Did you know that eating meat hurts, even destroys, the environment?**

Interviewer: I don't understand. How?

Cornfield: It is a fact that **rain forests in Central America are being destroyed to produce cheap beef to export to other countries,** including the United States. And that hamburger you like so much—well, it takes 20 square meters of rain forest for each burger!

Interviewer: Oh, no. But I don't like to eat tofu.

Cornfield: That's OK. There are other good foods to eat.

Interviewer: Well, we're almost out of time. Do you have any final comments?

Cornfield: There are many more interesting facts in my book. Think about this one before you order your next burger: In the last 300 years, Americans have cut down over half of their trees to get land to grow food to feed cattle—all because people think they need meat.

WHAT DO YOU THINK?

Which opinions do you agree with?
Check as many as you want.

❑ I think Americans eat too much meat, but people in other countries also eat more meat than before. I don't think it's good.

❑ Humans should give up eating meat. That way we get healthier, and we don't destroy the environment.

❑ It's impossible for me to give up meat. I enjoy eating hamburgers.

❑ We should avoid eating animal products like beef, pork, milk and eggs. It's better for us to eat just fish and vegetables.

❑ Maybe people should eat less meat, but I don't think we have to give it up completely.

Now exchange your ideas with a classmate.

TURN TO PAGE 80 FOR AN INTERACTION TIP.

LOOKING AT THE ISSUE

If you had to give up food made with animal products, which ones would you give up? What are your reasons?

	Would you give it up?	Why or why not?
hamburgers	yes / no	
steak	yes / no	
bacon	yes / no	
ice cream (milk, eggs)	yes / no	
pancakes (eggs, milk)	yes / no	
ham	yes / no	
chicken	yes / no	
pizza (cheese)	yes / no	
your idea:	yes / no	

Last Chance

This is a science fiction story about a woman from the year 2500.
She is talking to the leaders of the United Nations.
Read the story and find out: Why did she come to speak to them?

Good evening, ladies and gentlemen. Thank you all for coming here and listening to my story. Let me begin by telling you how I came to be here: **I came in a time machine.** In the year 2500, we are able to travel through time to any year in the history of the earth.

I have returned to this year to tell you something important: **This year is your last chance to change your lifestyle to save the earth!**

I will explain. Beginning in the middle of the 20th century, a few people were worried about polluting the earth's water and air. They talked about the dangers of pollution, but most people did not listen and did not change their way of life. Instead, they continued to dump dangerous chemicals and other waste into lakes and oceans, to drive more and more cars and trucks and to cut down trees.

By the year 2200, the earth's water was completely polluted. People could no longer drink water, and they had to use other types of liquids. This forced a change, but it was not enough. Scientists warned about over-population and said that in the future there might be too many people on the earth. But not enough was done.

So, by the year 2300, there were so many people that food became scarce. There was no water to grow food and all of the fish in the lakes and oceans died because of pollution. Terrible wars broke out between the wealthy and the poor. People started to think about finding another place to live. Scientists were working very hard to find another planet in space where humans could live.

By the year 2400, the air was too polluted for humans to breathe. So we had to leave earth. But only the very wealthy were able to leave. Where did we go? Nowhere. And everywhere. You see, scientists did not find another safe planet, so now we must travel around the universe in our space ships. We are still looking for a place to call our home.

So, it is up to you to change history. There is still hope. **You must change your lifestyle now, before it is too late.**

IN THE GLOSSARY (PAGE 90)
• *polluting the earth* • *dump* • *warn* • *population* • *scarce* • *broke out* • *wealthy*

WHAT DO YOU THINK?

What do you think about our modern lifestyle?
Check the opinions you agree with.

❏ We should definitely change our lifestyle. We should think about the environment more.

❏ I understand that we need to change, but I don't want to give up the comfortable and convenient life I have now.

❏ To tell the truth, I don't care. I won't be around in the future.

❏ We don't have to worry. Scientists always find answers to our problems.

❏ We have to start changing the way we live, little by little. Let's think about what we can do today.

Now exchange your ideas with a classmate.

TURN TO PAGE 81 FOR AN **INTERACTION TIP.**

LOOKING AT THE ISSUE

Here are suggestions for changing our lifestyle.
Do you think they are possible?

Suggestion	Yes, that's easy to do.	That's hard to do.	No, that's impossible to do.
Use less gasoline.			
Use solar or electric cars.			
Use less electricity (for example, don't stay up late at night).			
Eat less meat (this uses less forest land for cattle).			
Stop using disposable products.			
Recycle more.			
Control the population.			
your idea:			

Take the Money and **RUN**

Paulo Umberto is one of the world's best soccer players. Read the story and find out: Why is he thinking of moving to a new team?

Paulo Umberto is a lucky man. He is married to a wonderful woman and they have three healthy, happy children. He is also the best soccer player in his country. This past season he led his team, the Eagles, to the championship of his country.

The sportswriters say that the Eagles are the best team in the history of the country, and probably one of the best teams in the world. The Eagles do everything well—defense, passing and scoring. **Most everyone believes Paulo Umberto is the main reason for the success of the Eagles.**

But Paulo is thinking of leaving. His contract with the Eagles will end soon. So Paulo has been talking with the four owners of the team about a new contract. The four owners, all brothers whose family is very famous in the country, want very much to keep Paulo on the Eagles.

At the same time, **the owner of a famous English football team wants Paulo to play with his team.** He has offered Paulo a lot of money—much more than he earns now. If he signs with the English team, in five years he would make more money than he would earn in his lifetime playing in his country. He would be so rich that he would never have to worry about money again.

Paulo wants to continue to play for the Eagles and live in his own country. He really doesn't want to change his lifestyle and move to England. He doesn't speak English. His wife and his children want to stay in their country. He likes his teammates and the owners. He knows that they have offered him the best contract they can afford. No one is very wealthy in his country.

But the contract with the English team is very attractive. Paulo could help make that team the best in Europe, and maybe the world. And he would be very, very rich.

WHAT DO YOU THINK?

Do you think Paulo should "go for the money"?
Check the opinions you agree with.

❑ When there's a big chance, you should take it. Don't hesitate. You may never have a second big chance!

❑ Money and fame are exciting. If you can get them both, why not!

❑ I think you have to go for the money. You can never have too much money.

❑ Happiness is more important than money. You can't buy that with money.

❑ Peace and harmony are the most important things in life. If you have peace and harmony in your life, don't change, even for money.

Now exchange your ideas with a classmate.

TURN TO PAGE 81 FOR AN *INTERACTION TIP*.

LOOKING AT THE ISSUE

If you received a lot of money, what would you do? List three things.

1.   2.   3.

If you became very famous, how would you feel or what would you do?
List three things.

1.   2.   3.

Are there things money can't buy? List three things.

1.   2.   3.

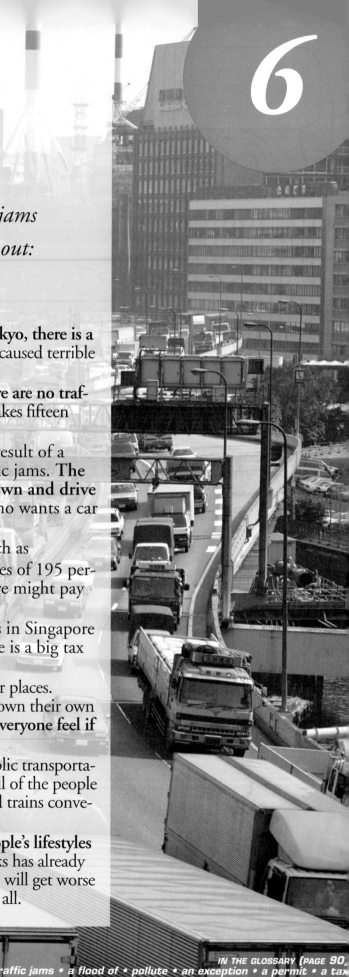

Traffic Jam

*In many countries, almost everyone
drives a car. But this means terrible traffic jams
and air pollution. Read this story and find out:
Why doesn't Singapore have a car problem?*

In many big Asian cities, such as Seoul, Taipei and Tokyo, there is a flood of cars, trucks and buses on the streets. This has caused terrible traffic jams that pollute the air.

One large city, Singapore, is an exception. There are no traffic jams. Its air is clean—free from pollution. It only takes fifteen minutes to drive from the city to the airport.

This happy situation is no accident. It is the result of a government program to fight air pollution and traffic jams. The government has simply made it very expensive to own and drive a car in Singapore. The program requires anyone who wants a car to buy a permit.

A 10-year permit to own a car can cost as much as US$75,000. And when you add sales and import taxes of 195 percent to the cost of buying a car, residents of Singapore might pay over US$250,000 to get a car and a permit.

In addition to the cost of owning a car, drivers in Singapore must pay to enter downtown on weekdays. And there is a big tax on gasoline.

As nice as this sounds, it might not work in other places. Think about your city. Think about how many people own their own cars and use them for work and pleasure. How would everyone feel if it became too expensive to own and drive cars?

There might be other problems. Would the public transportation system—the buses and trains—be able to handle all of the people who used to drive their own cars? And are the buses and trains convenient for everyone?

Clearly, something must be done to change people's lifestyles in the world's large cities. Pollution from cars and trucks has already caused serious damage to the earth's environment and it will get worse and worse. Perhaps Singapore has the right answer after all.

IN THE GLOSSARY (PAGE 90
• traffic jams • a flood of • pollute • an exception • a permit • a tax

WHAT DO YOU THINK?

What do you think about the car problem in large cities? Check the opinions you agree with.

❏ Other large cities should do what Singapore has done.

❏ What Singapore did is crazy. It's impossible to do in our city.

❏ We should do what Singapore has done, but only gradually, step by step.

❏ We should develop solar or electric cars. Then the problem of pollution will be gone.

❏ I understand the problem, but I just can't live without a car.

Now exchange your ideas with a classmate.

TURN TO PAGE 81 FOR AN INTERACTION TIP.

LOOKING AT THE ISSUE

Work with a partner. Ask your partner these questions:

Can you drive? Do you have a car? Does anybody in your family have a car? How do you go from your home to these places?

	Car	Bus	Taxi	Train	Subway	Walk	Bicycle
school							
work							
hospital							
shopping							
movies							
station							
post office							

SSUES IN FAMILY

- Does divorce hurt children?

- Should a couple stay married only for their children?

- A husband with two children worries about the future.

9

FOR THE SAKE OF THE CHILDREN

7

THE UNBORN CHILD

- What do you think about abortion?

- Is abortion ever necessary?

- A married couple has to make a difficult decision about their unborn child.

8

FAMILY HARMONY

- Is family harmony important?

- Should your family influence your decisions?

- A brother and sister disagree about a family decision.

10

FAMILY VALUES

- How do children learn to tell the truth?

- Is telling a lie ever a good idea?

- A mother teaches her child about the truth.

12

- How much should children help with housework?

- How should parents get children to cooperate?

- Two parents discuss a plan for their family.

A REWARD OR A BRIBE?

11

TAKING CARE OF MOTHER

- When an elderly parent cannot take care of herself, who should take care of her?

- Should an elderly parent move in with her children?

- A husband and wife disagree about taking care of the man's mother.

The Unborn Child

A wife and husband have to make a difficult decision.
Read the story and find out:
What are they trying to decide?

Sia and her husband, Ashat, have to make a very difficult decision. Sia, 38 years old, and Ashat, 42, have always wanted a child. They have been married for 10 years and tried for a long time to have a baby.

Now Sia is three months pregnant. Their doctor just told them that the fetus's brain is not developing properly. **If Sia gives birth, the baby will be badly handicapped, both mentally and physically.** It will always need special care and special schools.

Sia is depressed and confused. **She is against abortion and she really wants to have a baby now.** Three years ago, Sia was pregnant but lost the fetus in the fourth month. This pregnancy may be her last chance. She thinks she can love and take care of the baby, no matter how handicapped it might be.

While Ashat has always been opposed to abortion, he is having second thoughts. Ashat has a good job, and the health insurance from his company will pay for Sia's pregnancy. But it will not pay for all of the costs of the special care and schools that the child will need.

Ashat is worried about the future, after the baby is born. He wonders what kind of life it can have. **Ashat also wonders how a badly handicapped baby will change their lives.** Finally, **he is very worried about money**. They will not have enough money for the special care and schools.

What should they do? Should Sia have an abortion? Or should she have the baby and face the future then? But she must consider the feelings of her husband. Together they somehow must make a decision.

IN THE GLOSSARY (PAGE 91)
• *pregnant* • *fetus* • *developing* • *handicapped* • *mentally* • *physically* • *depressed* • *abortion*

WHAT DO YOU THINK?

Is abortion the right decision in this case?
Check the opinions you agree with.

❏ I think so. The baby has no future. Both the child and the parents will only suffer.

❏ Yes. Doctors don't know everything. Perhaps Sia will be able to have another baby.

❏ No, Sia should have the baby. All children, handicapped or normal, have the right to be born.

❏ No, an abortion is not the answer. This might be their last chance to have a baby.

❏ Miracles can happen. Maybe this baby will be fine. They should have the baby.

Now exchange your ideas with a classmate.

TURN TO PAGE 82 FOR AN INTERACTION TIP.

LOOKING AT THE ISSUE

Is abortion legal in your country?

completely legal   legal in some situations   completely illegal

In what situations should abortion be allowed? Check all that you agree with.

When the mother does not want the pregnancy

When the parents do not want the pregnancy

When the mother's health is in danger

When the pregnancy is because of rape

When the parents are very young

When the baby is going to be handicapped

It should never be allowed, regardless of the reasons.

FAMILY HARMONY

Mae and her brother Chew are very close, and they usually agree on everything. However, they have a disagreement now. Read this conversation and find out: What do they disagree about?

Mae: I just don't understand how you can think like that, Chew! It isn't like you at all.

Chew: **My wife and I simply want to send our daughter to a private school.** That's all. And you act like I've killed someone! What's the problem?

Mae: What about *my* daughter? You know **my husband and I don't have the money to send Wai to a private school.** She'll have to go to public school.

Chew: And why don't you have the money? Both you and Kuo have good jobs, just like my wife and I do.

Mae: You know why. We just bought a new house. **All of our money went to buy that new house.**

Chew: Fine. If buying a house is more important to you than education, that's your choice. We want our daughter to have the best education possible.

Mae: But think how Wai will feel when her cousin Shu-Ling goes to private school. **Those two girls are very close to one another.**

Chew: Yes, and I like that. But they'll still be close, even though they won't go to the same school.

Mae: It's not that simple. Your private school is much better than the public school Wai will go to.

Chew: **That's the reason we saved our money—so Shu-Ling can go to an excellent school.**

Mae: But think what will happen to the two girls. Now, because they're in the same class, they go to school together, take school trips

together and do their homework together.

Chew: That's right. Why didn't you think of that before you bought your new house?

Mae: Chew, listen to me. **Don't send Shu-Ling to private school. Don't separate them. Wai will be crushed.**

Chew: Perhaps, but she'll get over it.

IN THE GLOSSARY (PAGE 91)
• simply • public school • excellent • crushed • get over it

WHAT DO YOU THINK?

Which opinions do you agree with?
Check as many as you want.

❏ I think family harmony is important. You should give equal treatment to your children and close relatives.

❏ Each family should make its own decisions. They shouldn't worry about what their relatives say.

❏ If you don't get along with your close relatives, you'll be sorry. They'll talk about you all the time.

❏ Cousins don't need to be so close. They'll have different lives later, anyway.

❏ Life is hard, and we need our relatives to help us. We should do everything we can to stay close to them.

Now exchange your ideas with a classmate.

Turn to Page 82 for an INTERACTION TIP.

LOOKING AT THE ISSUE

Here are some cases in which people feel they are not treated fairly. What do you think?

	It's fair.	It's not fair.
Case 1: My older brother goes to a private university. My parents say I have to go to a public university because they don't have enough money for my education. But I want to go to a private university. It's not fair.	☐	☐
Case 2: My parents make me wash dishes, but my older sister gets out of it. Her job is taking out the trash, but that's much easier to do. My parents say she has more homework to do, so she shouldn't work too hard. I think it's unfair.	☐	☐
Case 3: My grandparents live with us. On New Year's, my cousins come to my house and at that time my grandparents give them more "gift money" than they give me. They say it's because they don't see my cousins very often. I think this is unfair.	☐	☐
Case 4: When my sister and her husband built their house, my parents gave them a lot of financial support. Now I want to buy a new condominium, but my parents say they can't help me financially. They say my sister has three children and needs more support, but I'm single and don't have a family. It's not fair.	☐	☐

Do you know any other examples like these?

For the Sake of the Children

Wali Abunit has not been healthy recently. Read his conversation with his doctor and find out: What is making him feel so bad?

"Wali, the results of the tests show that your blood pressure is high…too high for a man of your age. What's wrong?" asks Dr. Netaka.

"I don't know. Well, you know, I just don't feel happy. **I'm depressed.** Is that strange?"

"No, not at all. Unfortunately, many people are like that. Do you have any idea what's causing your depression?"

Wali hangs his head and stares at the floor. He is embarrassed. He starts to say something, but stops.

"Hmm," says his doctor. "I think you know what's wrong. You can tell me. I won't tell anyone else, not even your wife, Fionia."

"My wife…Fionia. It's funny that you should mention her name," says Wali. "Actually, **I think my marriage is the problem.** Did you know we've been married for 15 years? Fifteen long years," Wali sighs. "Our marriage is terrible. We fight and argue all the time. We can never agree on anything. It's hard for me to live with her. **I guess…I don't love my wife anymore.**"

"What about your two children? Do you love them?" asks Dr. Netaka.

"Yes, very much. And that's part of the problem. I'm afraid to get a divorce because of the children. **I think Fionia and I will have to stay married for the sake of the children.**"

Dr. Netaka thinks about this for a minute and then asks Wali, "Why? Why do you think you have to stay with your wife because of your children?"

"Everyone knows that **children suffer when their parents get divorced. I don't want my children to suffer and be unhappy and confused.** And I don't want to lose them. If I divorce Fionia, she will probably keep the children. I would only be able to see them every now and then. I couldn't bear that. I would miss them too much."

IN THE GLOSSARY (PAGE 91)
• *depressed* • *stares at* • *embarrassed* • *get a divorce* • *for the sake of* • *suffer* • *bear*

WHAT DO YOU THINK?

What do you think about divorce?
Check the opinions you agree with.

❏ Children don't want to see their parents unhappy or fighting all the time. So divorce may help the children, not hurt them.

❏ When parents get divorced, they should explain to their children that the divorce is the parents' problem and that the children are not to blame.

❏ Divorce is wrong. Husbands and wives should try hard to stay together.

❏ With or without children, it doesn't matter. When love ends, the marriage is over.

❏ It's OK to get divorced if you don't have children. But if you do have kids, you should never get divorced.

Now exchange your ideas with a classmate.

TURN TO PAGE 82 FOR AN INTERACTION TIP.

LOOKING AT THE ISSUE

In many countries, the divorce rate is getting higher and higher. Is there a way to lower it? Check the ideas you like.

The government gives money as a reward to couples who have been married for a long time.

Divorce is not allowed, except in certain situations, such as terrible mental illness.

The government charges a high tax on divorces.

The government hires marriage counselors to give advice to people.

Couples live together for a few years before they decide to get married.

Couples live together but don't get married.

What are your ideas?

1.

2.

3.

Family Values

Mi-Yeon remembers something important that happened when she was a little girl. Read the story and find out: What happened? What did she learn?

I was in the kitchen helping my mother when I heard the crash. I knew at once what had happened. I turned and started to run toward the room where the guests were, but my mother stopped me.

"Wait," she said. "**Let's return to our guests as if nothing has happened. Do not show how upset and angry you are.**"

"But Mother, how can you say that? You know what has happened. Our family vase has been broken. You heard the crash. This is terrible."

My mother smiled at me and replied, "Yes, I know. **The vase that has been in our family for over 200 years is broken.** But we mustn't let our guests know how priceless it is."

With that, she picked up the tea, and we returned to our guests. When we entered the room, I saw at once that my worst fear was right—the priceless vase was in pieces on the floor. And standing next to the broken vase was the 4-year-old son of Mrs. Kim.

Mrs. Kim had a horrified look on her face.

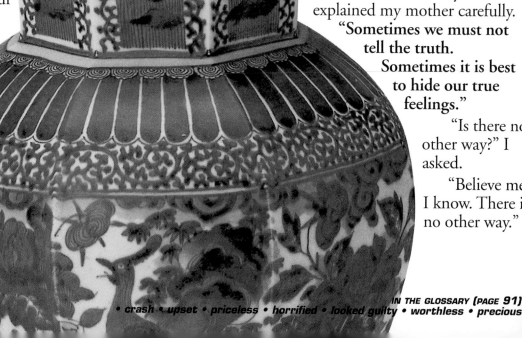

The boy was starting to cry. He looked very guilty.

"I...I...well, somehow...," Mrs. Kim began to explain

My mother quickly said, "**Oh, that's all right. It was an old vase. It was not valuable.**"

"But the vase just fell off the shelf," Mrs. Kim replied

"Oh, don't worry about it. Everything is just fine. Would you like some tea? And what about some of these sweets?"

After our guests had gone, I asked my mother "Why did you say that the vase was worthless? You know that it was very valuable."

"What else could I say?" my mother replied. "Could I say it was valuable? That the boy had broken our family's most precious treasure? Could I say that?"

"Well," I said, "It's the truth. **We should always tell the truth.**" "Not always," explained my mother carefully. "**Sometimes we must not tell the truth. Sometimes it is best to hide our true feelings.**"

"Is there no other way?" I asked.

"Believe me I know. There i no other way."

WHAT DO YOU THINK?

What was the mother trying to teach her daughter?
Check the sentences you agree with.

❏ Relationships with people are more important than material things like vases.

❏ Other people's feelings are more important than your own feelings.

❏ It's sometimes necessary to tell a lie.

❏ Never show other people your true feelings, especially sadness or anger.

❏ Don't embarrass other people. Always protect their feelings.

Now exchange your ideas with a classmate.

TURN TO PAGE 83 FOR AN INTERACTION TIP.

LOOKING AT THE ISSUE

Here are some values we might learn from our families.
Which are the most important in your culture?

Always tell the truth.

Always protect other people's feelings.

Never speak badly about someone else.

Show respect, especially to older people.

Never let anyone see your true feelings, especially if you are hurt or sad.

Always help others who need your help.

What other values did you learn in your family?

Taking Care of Mother

Toshi is worried about his 78-year-old mother. Read Toshi's conversation with his wife, Midori, and find out: What do they want to do for his mother?

Toshi: We have to face the facts. **Mother is too old to live alone.**

Midori: Yes, you're probably right. She is getting older, and since your father died, she seems very forgetful.

Toshi: Mother will need someone to take care of her in the near future.

Midori: Perhaps we could hire a nurse. You know, someone who could come in during the day, clean the house, cook some meals, make sure she takes her pills.

Toshi: But nurses don't do all of those things. You're thinking of a nurse and a housekeeper. Who would pay for that? **It will be very expensive!**

Midori: Well, Toshi, what are you thinking?

Toshi: Since I'm the only child, we have to take care of her. She can come to live with us.

Midori: Here? **In this tiny house? There are only two bedrooms.** We can't move our two daughters out of their small bedroom.

Toshi: What else can we do? We can't afford to hire a nurse and a housekeeper. I'm her only child. Her husband, brother and sister are all dead. We have to take care of her.

Midori: Maybe we could look for a bigger house.

Toshi: In Tokyo? You know that's impossible. We tried looking last year and everything in this area of Tokyo is too expensive.

Midori: Let's move away from the city. Someplace cheap.

Toshi: But then I would be far away from my office. It might take me two or three hours on the train. I hate to commute. No, the only solution is for Mother to live with us here.

IN THE GLOSSARY (PAGE 91)
• forgetful • hire • a housekeeper • pills • tiny • commute • solution

WHAT DO YOU THINK?

Which opinions do you agree with?
Check as many as you want.

❏ It's too expensive to take care of old people. I think the government should be responsible for taking care of them.

❏ Taking care of elderly parents is the child's duty. So the child should not depend on other people or on the government for help.

❏ Your parents should live with you when they're old, even if your house is small.

❏ If your mother or father suddenly comes to your house to live, it will cause a lot of problems.

❏ Elderly people should live in special homes. They shouldn't bother their children.

Now exchange your ideas with a classmate.

TURN TO PAGE 83 FOR AN INTERACTION TIP.

LOOKING AT THE ISSUE

Many older parents live with their children. Can you think of reasons for and against this arrangement?

Older parents should live with their children because...

It's more fun with more members in the family.

Older parents should not live with their children because...

My small house would be crowded.

A **Reward** or a *BRIBE?*

*Kimo and Makana have two boys, ages 10 and 14.
They are having a difficult time getting the boys to help
around the house. Read their conversation and find out:
What are they planning to do?*

Kimo: I'm so tired of asking Kam and Tasama to do their tasks. **They never do anything.** They say they forgot or they were too busy with homework.

Makana: I know what you mean. Yesterday, I was so mad at Kam because he didn't make his bed that I almost hit him.

Kimo: Not a good idea! **We've already discussed hitting the children, and neither of us believes that it's a good idea.**

Makana: I know, but what else can we do?

Kimo: I asked my brother for his advice this morning. **He suggested that we pay the children to work around the house.**

Makana: What? Pay them for doing what they should do? Never!

Kimo: Well, that was what I thought. But my brother told me about a plan that has worked in other families.

Makana: How does it work? I'm willing to try almost anything.

Kimo: **First we make a list of things that the boys have to do each day and during the week.** You know, keep their room clean, make their beds, take out the trash, and so on. We put it on the refrigerator so everyone can see it.

Makana: OK, what next?

Kimo: **Then we tell Kam and Tasama that they'll get a certain amount of money each week if they do all of their tasks. But if they don't do all of the tasks, then they'll get no money.** Nothing at all.

Makana: Do you mean if the boys miss one task, they get no money?

Kimo: Right. Then they wouldn't have any money for going to the movies or buying comics or anything.

Makana: Well, I don't know. **That plan seems like a bribe to me.**

Kimo: **Think of it as a reward!**

IN THE GLOSSARY (PAGE 91)
• *tasks* • *trash* • *miss* • *a bribe* • *a reward*

WHAT DO YOU THINK?

Which opinions do you agree with?
Check as many as you want.

❏ Children should do some things for free, like cleaning their own room. But they should be paid to do other tasks like washing dishes.

❏ Parents should pay their children to do housework. And that should be the only money they get. That way, they learn to be responsible.

❏ Helping around the house is something children have to do. They shouldn't get paid for it.

❏ Paying the children to do housework is a bribe. Don't do it. They'll start asking for money for everything.

❏ Giving money for doing housework is a reward. Children need rewards for doing things.

Now exchange your ideas with a classmate.

TURN TO PAGE 83 FOR AN INTERACTION TIP.

LOOKING AT THE ISSUE

In your house, who does the following tasks?

	me	my brother/sister	my mother	my father	my grandparent(s)
cleaning the house					
cleaning your room					
laundry					
washing dishes					
shopping for food					
taking out the trash					

SSUES IN RELATIONSHIPS

- Should people keep pets?
- What's the best way to treat pets
- A cat tells the story of his difficult life with his owner.

14

TOM CAT'S STORY

13

FRIENDS AND LOVERS?

- What is a "best friend"?
- Is it possible for men and women to be best friends?
- A young man and woman suddenly have to ask this question.

15

AN INTERNATIONAL RELATIONSHIP

- Can people from different countries be good friends?
- What issues does an international couple have to face?
- A university student has fallen in love with someone from another country.
  She wonders what the future with him could be like.

Friends and *Lovers?*

Keiko and Akira have been friends for a long time. But something has happened, and they might not be friends any longer. Read the story and find out: What has happened to hurt, and maybe even end, their friendship?

Akira and Keiko leave the university library after several hours of studying together, something they do often. Suddenly, **Akira tries to kiss Keiko**. Keiko is shocked.

"What are you doing, Akira?" Keiko asks, hardly able to speak. "**You're my best friend. We've been friends** for five years. You're closer to me than my brother. And now you want to kiss me?"

Akira explains, "**I want our friendship to be even closer.**"

"No, no, no! I don't think of you in that way. You're my friend. **Best friends don't act that way.**"

Akira looks confused. "I don't understand. Don't you see me as a man?"

"Of course I do," replies Keiko. "You're a handsome man. But you're a special man...my best

friend. So we can't do this. Now do you understand?"

"No, not at all. Here is how I see it. You're a woman and I'm a man. We like each other very much. We're very close. **So let's do what is natural in any male-female relationship.**"

"Natural? I think our friendship is natural. I thought I understood you. Maybe I was wrong," cries Keiko.

Akira's face is red. "So you really don't like me at all. You just want someone to talk to." He turns and walks quickly away.

Keiko's anger turns to sadness. In her heart, she thinks Akira is wrong—**men and women can be friends without being lovers.** But now she's not sure. What if all men think like Akira?

IN THE GLOSSARY (PAGE 92)
• shocked • replies

WHAT DO YOU THINK?

Can a man and a woman be close friends without being lovers? Check the opinions you agree with.

❏ Sometimes they can be friends, but usually friendship between a man and a woman is difficult.

❏ Maybe not. If a man and a woman are close friends, they will naturally become lovers.

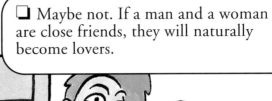

❏ Yes, they can. I know a lot of cases like that among my friends.

❏ It's impossible, because men always want to have sex with women they like.

❏ Of course they can. I have some good men friends and we're just friends.

Now exchange your ideas with a classmate.

TURN TO PAGE 84 FOR AN INTERACTION TIP.

LOOKING AT THE ISSUE

• What is your best friend like? Use three adjectives.

For example, *tall, kind, talkative.*

She (He) is _____, _____ *and* _____.

• Why is that person your best friend?

For example, *She helps me when I'm in trouble.*
We have a great time talking together.

1.

2.

3.

• Is your best friend a man or a woman?

Tom Cat's Story

14

Some pets have a hard life. Read this story and find out:
What is this cat's problem?

My name is Tom and I am a cat. I have a major problem whose name is Felina. Felina is my owner. **You see, she doesn't understand how people should take care of their pets. She has very strange ideas about the relationship between people and pets.**

Felina treats me like a human child. She worries about me and tells me what to do all of the time. She doesn't want me to go outside and play with the other cats. She makes me sit on her lap every night while she watches television. Boring. And the programs she watches! No taste at all!

There's more. **Felina brushes and combs me twice a day.** She takes me to the Pet Beauty Clinic once a week for a bath and shampoo. Really. Cats can take care of themselves. Doesn't she know that we have tongues that we use to lick ourselves and keep clean? And the flea powder she puts on me—it smells awful and I think it might give me skin cancer.

Felina thinks she knows what kind of food I like. She doesn't even have a clue. She feeds me this gourmet cat food and she puts it in a silver dish.

Really! Who cares? All I want is some day-old fish that stinks. And a little water. That's all. Is that asking too much?

One time I managed to get out of the house. Did I have a good time! I ran around with some other cats in the neighborhood. We ate garbage and chased a dog. I even killed a bird and ate it. Good fun. But when I returned home, Felina went crazy. She was so angry. She took me right to the Pet Beauty Clinic for a bath and shampoo, even though I had just been there the day before.

Once I had a relationship with a real sexy Siamese down the street, but Felina stopped it. Then **Felina got me fixed. Now I can't be a father and have children,** and I have lost all of my interest in female cats.

To make matters even worse, **she wants to have me buried next to her!** I won't be free of her even when I am dead. What a life.

IN THE GLOSSARY (PAGE 92)
• treats • lap • flea powder • doesn't have a clue • gourmet
• stinks • managed to get out • chased • got me fixed • buried

WHAT DO YOU THINK?

What do you think about pets?
Check the opinions you agree with.

❏ People should respect animal rights. Owning a pet doesn't mean you can do anything you want.

❏ People need pets for emotional support. I think they're great.

❏ People should not keep pets. They don't belong in people's homes.

❏ People treat pets too much like humans. I think it's silly.

❏ People spend too much money on pets. What a waste! Think of all the homeless people in the world.

Now exchange your ideas with a classmate.

TURN TO PAGE 84 FOR AN _INTERACTION TIP._

LOOKING AT THE ISSUE

Work with a partner. Ask these questions.

- Do you have a pet?
  (Yes) What do you have? What's its name? What is it like?
  (No) Are you interested in keeping a pet? What kind?

- What's good about keeping pets? What are the problems?

Good points	Bad points
They comfort us.	_They smell._

- Which pet is the easiest to keep? Which is the most difficult to keep?

a cat   a dog   a bird   a hamster   a goldfish   a rabbit

AN INTERNATIONAL RELATIONSHIP

Sachiko is a 22-year-old Japanese student who is spending her senior year at an American university in Los Angeles. She has met a special man named Amir. Read her diary and find out: What is she trying to decide?

Dear Diary,

Tonight **Amir asked me to marry him**! I knew he would. I love him so much. It is hard to believe that we have known each other for only eight months.

But as much as I love him, I don't know what to do. **My parents would be angry with me for marrying a man from India. They want me to marry only a Japanese man.** My mother has told me that good Japanese marry only Japanese.

And that's not all. **There are so many other problems.** I mean, where would we live? **I think it would be very hard for me to live in India.** Would I fit in to Indian society? I don't speak any Indian languages. I would have a difficult time finding a job. And I don't want to be just a housewife! That's for sure.

I don't think Amir would fit in to Japanese society, either. He doesn't speak Japanese. He sounds so funny when he tries to say a single Japanese word! It would be impossible for him to find a job in Japan. Besides, he doesn't even like Japanese food!

Maybe we could stay in the United States. Both of us will finish our studies in May.

I wonder if we could get work visas here. That might be difficult. But even if we could stay here, I don't know if I want to live away from Japan. I would miss my family and friends and everything.

And what about our children? **Children of mixed marriages might have a difficult time.** Would they be Japanese? Indian? What? It is all so confusing.

The more I write to you, dear diary, the more problems I see. I know that marriage is difficult. More and more marriages end in divorce. **And I think that international marriages are even more difficult!**

Oh, I am SO confused.

IN THE GLOSSARY (PAGE 92)
• *fit in • miss • mixed marriages • confusing*

15

WHAT DO YOU THINK?

What should Sachiko do?
Check the responses you agree with.

❏ They shouldn't make a decision about marriage right now. They should visit each other's country. There is a lot of time to think about what to do.

❏ She should marry Amir and live in the U.S. That's fair for both Amir and her. Both of them could visit their home countries sometimes.

❏ She should marry Amir and try living in India. It could be a really good experience for her.

❏ Sachiko should break up with Amir. There are too many problems to continue the relationship.

❏ She should marry Amir and live in Japan. More and more foreign people are living in Japan, so Amir will be accepted.

Now exchange your ideas with a classmate.

TURN TO PAGE 84 FOR AN INTERACTION TIP.

LOOKING AT THE ISSUE

What are some of the advantages of an international marriage?

1.
2.
3.

What are some of the problems with an international marriage?

1.
2.
3.

20 Years of Pain

16

Abi and Moon had been married for 20 years. They had four children. Then one day, Abi killed Moon. Read the story and find out:
Why did she murder her husband?

Abi L. is a small woman with a gentle smile. She speaks quietly and politely. She seems like the nice woman who lives next door, not the kind of person who is in prison for murdering her husband. Abi tells her story carefully, how the problem began, **how after 20 years of pain she finally killed her husband.**

Abi explains: "**Before we were married, Moon was the nicest, most gentle man I had ever met.** Maybe that is why I married him. He was so kind. The first two years were wonderful. **But then something happened.** He started working late, not coming home, and drinking a lot."

She continues, speaking softly, "At first, when he was angry, he just pushed me. Then later he kicked me or slapped my face a few times. **After a while he started to beat me badly.** Once he choked me so hard I thought I was going to die."

Abi looks down at her hands. They still have scars from the time her husband pushed her through a window. The hands are small but strong enough to reach for a kitchen knife and stab her husband to death. This is what Abi did last June when her husband began to beat her again.

Wife-beating happens more often than most people know. Not just here, but all over the world. In some societies, men believe it is their right to beat their wives. And though there are laws against attacking people, most men who hurt their wives are not punished.

The reason? **Most women say nothing when beaten.** Abi did not tell her relatives or friends. She did not even call the police. Abi explains: "The police do nothing. If a woman calls the police, her husband can just give them money, and they'll leave. Then he'll beat his wife more and more."

Abi is now in prison, awaiting trial for murder. **Her friends say she should go free. They believe she killed Moon in self-defense. Others say she must pay for her crime with her own life.**

Abi's eyes are sad and tired. "I don't know what will happen now. All I know is that I killed my husband because I didn't know what else to do."

IN THE GLOSSARY (PAGE 92)
• murdering • kicked • slapped • choked • scars • stab • right • punished • trial • in self-defense

WHAT DO YOU THINK?

What do you think should happen to Abi?
Check the opinions you agree with.

❑ She suffered a lot, but it is wrong to kill a person. She should stay in jail for the rest of her life.

❑ She killed her husband in self-defense, so she should not be punished.

❑ She suffered long enough. She should go free.

❑ It was right for her to kill her husband. He deserved to die.

❑ It's simple. Abi killed her husband, so she should pay with her life.

Now exchange your ideas with a classmate.

TURN TO PAGE 85 FOR AN INTERACTION TIP.

LOOKING AT THE ISSUE

Which of these ideas can help to stop violence by men against women? Which will not? Why or why not?

will help   won't help

There should be strict laws to protect women.

Women need to learn how to defend themselves. They need to fight back when they are beaten.

Men who beat women should go to jail for a long time.

Men need to be educated about violence to change their thinking and behavior.

We need to stop violence all over the world, not just between husbands and wives.

How can we reduce violence in the world?
For example, stop showing violent scenes on TV.

1.   2.   3.

Happily Ever After

17

This is a story about two people, Jasmine and Samuel. It has three endings. Read and find out: What happens to them? Which relationship do you like?

The Beginning: At a party one night in March, a friend of Jasmine's introduces her to Samuel. **Samuel and Jasmine fall in love and get married.**

Relationship 1: Jasmine and Samuel both have interesting and exciting jobs. Early in their relationship they decide not to have children. Instead, they spend all of their time on their work and careers. Over time, **they are both very successful and very rich. They spend very little time together, finding happiness in their work.** They enjoy having large and expensive parties in their big home. They live happily ever after.

Relationship 2: Samuel is an accountant in an office near their small house. He earns a good salary, but they will never be wealthy. But Samuel and Jasmine don't care. **They are not interested in money. They don't have children, but that doesn't matter. All they need is each other.** When Samuel is finished with work, he goes straight home, where Jasmine is waiting for him. Jasmine doesn't work outside the home. She spends her time housekeeping and cooking and helping her husband. As time goes by, Jasmine and Samuel remain deeply in love. They live happily ever after.

Relationship 3: Both Jasmine and Samuel want a lot of children, even though his job as an office clerk doesn't pay much money. So they have six children. **Jasmine and Samuel are wonderful parents. They spend all the time they can with their children and with each other.** Samuel was offered a promotion to office manager, but he refused. He thought it would take too much time, and he wanted to be with his wife and children as much as possible. They have very little money and very few things. But they have each other and their children. They live happily ever after.

IN THE GLOSSARY (PAGE 92)
• over time • an accountant • remain• a promotion • refused

WHAT DO YOU THINK?

Which relationship do you like?
Check the idea you agree with.

❏ It is important for each person in a relationship to have an interesting job and do well. Everything else is unimportant, including children.

❏ It is important for couples to have a happy marriage and children. Money or jobs are not important.

❏ It is important for couples to love each other deeply and to find happiness in their relationship. That is enough. Money, children and jobs are not important.

Now exchange your ideas with a classmate.

TURN TO PAGE 85 FOR AN *INTERACTION TIP.*

LOOKING AT THE ISSUE

What is important for your ideal marriage or relationship?
Check as many as you like. Then add some of your own ideas.

love	☐	no children	☐
a good income	☐	one or two children	☐
being wealthy	☐	three children or more	☐
an interesting job	☐	a big house	☐
success in my job	☐	living in one place	☐
both partners having jobs	☐	living in different places	☐
a good family life	☐	having a lot of friends	☐
being/having a full-time housewife	☐	having a lot of parties	☐

your own ideas:

1.

2.

3.

4.

GROWING APART

18

Okenoy is having problems with his best friend. Read the story and find out: What is causing the problems?

Kwan is my best friend. I mean, he and I have always been very close. We're the same age, 21. We went to the same high school and now attend the same university. We are both English majors and want to be English teachers after we graduate. When we were growing up, we always did a lot of things together—baseball, music lessons and club activities in high school.

Even more important, we always talked to each other, sharing our highs and our lows, our fears and our secret wishes. I will always remember and treasure that closeness.

But something has changed. Kwan and I are not as close as before; I think **we are slowly growing apart.** I tried to talk to Kwan about it, but he said there was no change. Actually, he really didn't want to talk about it and cut me off.

And it's not just that. **His behavior has changed.** Now he stays out late at night and doesn't get home until 3 or 4 in the morning. Of course, this means that he sleeps late and often misses classes. I know we don't have much homework, but I don't see him studying at all. And he has missed the last five meetings of the English club.

I'm worried, really worried. A friend of ours hinted last week that Kwan was in trouble. I questioned him about it, but he didn't want to tell me anything. I begged him to tell me, and finally he said that **maybe Kwan is taking drugs.**

I was shocked! I got angry and told my friend he was wrong and that he should stop telling lies about Kwan. But later I cooled down and thought about what he had told me. And the more I thought about it, the more I realized what he said could be true. I mean, Kwan has been acting very strange.

I wish I knew what to do.

WHAT DO YOU THINK?

What would you do if you were Kwan's friend? Check the best answer.

❏ I wouldn't worry. Maybe Kwan has a girlfriend who keeps him out late.

❏ I would talk to Kwan again. I would tell him, "I'm really worried about you."

❏ I would ask Kwan if he's taking drugs and see his reaction.

❏ I would not do anything at this point. I would wait and see what happens.

❏ I would talk to my parents and ask them what to do.

Now exchange your ideas with a classmate.

TURN TO PAGE 85 FOR AN INTERACTION TIP.

LOOKING AT THE ISSUE

What can best friends do? Check your answers.

Lend each other money

Borrow money from each other

Lend each other books

Lend their cars to each other

Introduce boyfriends or girlfriends to each other

Invite each other to their homes

Tell each other secrets

Talk about sex

Share a drink from the same glass

Ask for advice on a serious problem

your ideas:

•   •

SSUES IN LIFE AND DEATH

- Do people have the right to end their own life?

- Is it a crime to help someone die?

- A dying man, with help from his doctors, decides to take his own life.

21

THE RIGHT TO DIE

19

FLIGHT 77

- Do you believe in "fate"?

- Do you think some people have a special sense for avoiding danger?

- A traveler hears a voice that saves his life.

20

DOING THE RIGHT THING

- Should patients know about their medical condition?

- How can we help a dying patient?

- A daughter wants to do the right thing.

- What should we do if our lives are threatened?

- Is saving lives more important than anything?

- A passenger on a hijacked plane tells his story.

24

HOSTAGE

22

ALIVE OR DEAD?

- What happens when we die?

- Can we die and then come back to life?

- A bike rider was killed. Or was she?

23

SHOULD THE DEAD HELP THE LIVING?

- Should we donate our organs to help save lives?

- Why doesn't everyone think it is a good idea?

- Three doctors discuss this issue.

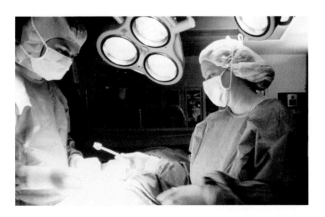

FLIGHT 77

19

*Joe had an experience that brought
him close to death. Read the story and find out:
What saved Joe's life?*

Something really weird happened to me. Let me say that I am a young man, 25 years old, with both feet on the ground. Which is to say that **I am an ordinary guy, not very different from everyone else.**

I am a salesman. I put in a lot of time traveling around the country trying to sell men's clothing—you know, shirts, pants, sweaters, that sort of thing.

This particular day, I am in Toronto and have to fly to Vancouver. No big deal. I am at the airport, waiting to get on my plane. It is a beautiful day. Not a cloud in the sky. **But I get this funny feeling about that flight to Vancouver. It is like I hear a voice in my head, saying that I should not get on that plane.**

Now I am just an ordinary guy—I am not the kind of person who hears voices or sees things that aren't there. At first, I don't pay much attention. **But as I walk toward the gate, this weird feeling gets worse and worse. It won't go away.** It's like I hear someone saying in my ear, "Don't get on that plane. Don't get on that plane."

I look around. Everything is OK. Everybody is fine. The other passengers are in line, getting on the plane.

I ask you, what would you do?

Well, I turn around, walk back to the ticket counter and buy a ticket for another flight.

You know the rest of the story. That's right. **The Vancouver plane—the one I didn't take—crashed into the side of a mountain, killing everyone on board.** One hundred twenty-one people. Dead.

I can't believe what happened. I was saved. But how?

WHAT DO YOU THINK? How do you explain the "inner voice" that Joe heard? Check the opinions you agree with.

❏ Maybe it was Joe's dead father or some ancestor who is always with him, protecting him.

❏ Joe probably has a sixth sense. You know, he can sense things that are going to happen, kind of like a fortune teller.

❏ It was just a feeling, just luck. Nothing more.

❏ I think it was God's voice. God wanted to save Joe.

❏ I believe in angels. I think Joe has an angel who is watching over him.

Now exchange your ideas with a classmate.

TURN TO PAGE 86 FOR AN INTERACTION TIP.

LOOKING AT THE ISSUE Some people believe they have a "sixth sense" to help them do things like:

- know what's going to happen in the future
- read other people's minds
- see through things
- move things without touching them

If there is such a thing as a sixth sense ("ESP"), would you want to have it?

Yes

I want the power to

Then I would

For example: I want to know what's going to happen in the future. Then I would prevent big accidents and the world would be safe.

No,

I don't want any of those powers because

Doing the *RIGHT* Thing

Yumi needs advice about a problem involving her father.
She has written to Dr. Aoki, a famous medical counselor.
Read the story and find out: What does Yumi want to tell her father?

Dear Dr. Aoki,

My name is Yumi. I'm a 19-year-old college student. Something terrible is happening and I don't know what to do. Please help me.

My father is dying. According to his doctor, he has only three more months to live. He has stomach cancer, which has now spread to other parts of his body. Because the cancer has spread, it is too late for an operation. The doctor says there is nothing we can do.

I am heartbroken. But what is more painful to me is that **my father does not know about his disease. His doctor told him that he has an ulcer. My mother is trying to hide the fact as well.** They are both lying to him.

I think they are wrong. **I think my father has the right to know about his disease.** He should be informed. But when I told my mother that we should tell my father the truth, her eyes filled with tears. She said, "I don't think so, Yumi. If we tell him that he is going to die soon, he will be so shocked, depressed and upset that it might even shorten his life. We should not take hope away from him."

I understand that. However, I still think my father should know what's happening to him. It's his body. It's his life. Of course he would be shocked at first. But I'm sure he has things he would like to do before he dies, and he should be able to use whatever time he has left.

What do you think I should do? Should I persuade my mother to change her mind? Should I talk to the doctor? If they don't change their minds, should I tell my father? Or is my mother right after all? Please, please tell me what to do. I love my father very much and I want to do the right thing.

Sincerely,

Yumi Sato

• cancer • an operation • heartbroken • an ulcer • disease • be informed • shorten • persuade

WHAT DO YOU THINK?

If a patient is dying, should the doctor inform him or her? Check the ideas you agree with.

❑ No. You can't tell someone he or she is going to die. The patient will be too shocked. You shouldn't take away their hope.

❑ It depends. If the patient is mentally strong, he or she should be informed.

❑ It depends. The doctor should ask the patient's family.

❑ Yes. The patient should be able to use whatever time he or she has left.

❑ Yes. The patient has the right to know about his or her disease.

Now exchange your ideas with a classmate.

TURN TO PAGE 86 FOR AN INTERACTION TIP.

LOOKING AT THE ISSUE

What rights do you think patients should have? Do patients have these rights in your country?

Should have? Yes/No	Patients should have the right...	In my country? Yes/No
☐	to be informed about their disease.	☐
☐	to see all of their medical records.	☐
☐	to have an explanation about how the doctor will treat their disease.	☐
☐	to know the doctor's name and background.	☐
☐	to get a second opinion from another doctor.	☐
☐	to change doctors or hospitals.	☐
☐	to be involved in the decision on how to treat their disease.	☐
☐	not to be informed about their disease.	☐

The Right to Die

Keoni Tabido has made a decision. Read the story and find out: Why does he want to end his life?

Keoni Tabido has planned how he will spend his final hours: He will have a party for his friends, with lots of food, drink and music. Later, he will spend time with his girlfriend. And then, at midnight, **he will take a deadly mixture of drugs.**

Mr. Tabido is not crazy. He is a 33-year-old businessman. He is very successful, has a lot of money and enjoys life.

But **Mr. Tabido has a terrible disease.** This disease kills the nerve cells in his brain and spinal cord, slowly paralyzing him. Gradually, it will be difficult for him to swallow and breathe. **There is no cure for this deadly disease.**

So, after a great deal of thought, Mr. Tabido has decided to kill himself. He has told his family and friends about his plan. He has even bought a wooden coffin in which he will be buried.

"I don't want to become a vegetable, kept alive on a life-support machine," Mr. Tabido says. "I can't imagine anything worse. So I have planned my own death. I will do it while I can think and act clearly. I want to go out doing what I love best —having a good time."

In Mr. Tabido's country, it is against the law to help people die. If anyone, even a doctor, helps somebody to die, regardless of how sick or old that person is, they could be put in prison for 20 years.

Mr. Tabido is trying to make sure no one is punished for helping him die. **"Two doctors have helped me,"** says Mr. Tabido. "But I will never tell anyone their names. These doctors have given me the drugs and showed me how to inject myself. I will have only one chance, so I have to do it right the first time."

"I know that some people think it is wrong to kill yourself, and for others to help you. But they don't have a disease like mine. **For me, there is no choice."**

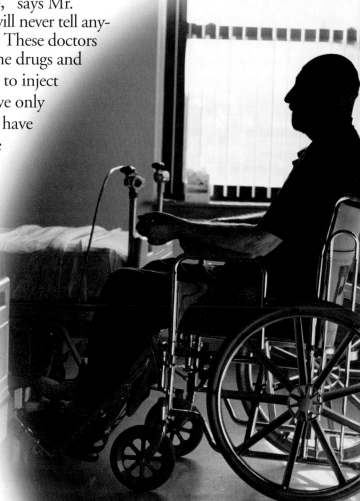

• *a deadly mixture of drugs* • *nerve cells* • *spinal cord* • *paralyzing* • *gradually* • *a coffin* • *become a vegetable* • *regardless*

WHAT DO YOU THINK? Do you think what Mr. Tabido and his doctors are doing is right? Check your opinion.

❏ In this case, I think suicide is all right. But his doctors should not help. Doctors should cure people, not kill them!

❏ If someone wants to die, that's their business. And if they need a doctor's help, that's fine, too.

❏ Yes. Suicide is OK in this kind of situation. It's cruel to stop it.

❏ No. It's wrong to take your own life. Mr. Tabido shouldn't give up.

❏ Well, we have to respect Mr. Tabido's decision, even if we don't agree with it.

Now exchange your ideas with a classmate.

TURN TO PAGE 86 FOR AN INTERACTION TIP.

LOOKING AT THE ISSUE

Suppose some scientists invent medicine to help people live forever. One day they come to you and say, "If you take the medicine in this bottle, you will never get old and you will never die." Would you take it? Why or why not?

Yes, I would take it because:

No, I wouldn't take it because:

ALIVE or Dead?

Toby is in the hospital recovering from a bicycle accident.
Read her conversation with her husband and find out:
What does she remember about the accident?

Ellis: Toby, do you feel like talking now? You've been in the hospital for three days without saying much.

Toby: I know, Ellis. I've been afraid to say anything. **I'm afraid everyone will think I'm crazy** or that my brain has been damaged or something like that.

Ellis: What do you mean? You're fine. All of the tests show that you're OK. You broke your leg, but otherwise no permanent damage.

Toby: Yes, I know. But something strange happened to me. If I tell you, will you promise not to tell anyone else?

Ellis: Of course, honey. I'll keep it a secret.

Toby: OK, here goes: **I remember being hit by the car. Then I was floating, weightless, about five meters above my body, looking down at my poor broken body.** I didn't feel any pain. Actually, it was a very pleasant sensation.

Ellis: Wow! That is strange. What happened then?

Toby: I could see a crowd looking at my body. A man began to breathe into my mouth, trying to get me to breathe. I heard the wail of an ambulance as it arrived at the scene. Just then, the man who was breathing into my mouth stopped, stood up, and shrugged his shoulders. He had given up. **I was dead.**

Ellis: And you saw all of this, from above your body?

Toby: Yes, but I felt no emotion. That dead body on the road had no connection with me. I had left it behind and was free. I watched as one of the men from the ambulance opened his bag and pulled out a needle and filled it

from a bottle. Then he injected it straight into my heart. **The next thing I knew I was back in my body, feeling the terrible pain and weight of a smashed body.** The man shouted, "It worked! She's breathing! She's alive!"

Ellis: Oh, my gosh. Yes, they told me that. They said you were very near death. Well, it's OK now. Don't worry, I won't tell anyone.

IN THE GLOSSARY (PAGE 93)
• *recovering* • *floating* • *weightless* • *a sensation* • *wail*
• *an ambulance* • *shrugged his shoulders* • *given up* • *emotion* • *a smashed body*

❏ Yes. This is a typical near-death experience. I know someone who had an experience like this.

❏ No! It's total nonsense. Maybe Toby's brain was damaged in the accident.

❏ I'm not sure. I don't understand how it could happen.

❏ No. Toby's probably confused because of the drugs and medicine she was given.

❏ Yes. I've heard stories about the same experience, and I believe them.

Now exchange your ideas with a classmate.

TURN TO PAGE 87 FOR AN INTERACTION TIP.

LOOKING AT THE ISSUE   What do you think happens when a person dies? Why do you think so?

When a person dies, that's it. There is nothing else. Life is over.

When a person dies, he or she will come back to life in a different form: as an insect, an animal or another person.

When a person dies, the body is dead but the soul is alive and goes to a different world.

I don't agree with any of those ideas. Here's what I think happens:

Should the Dead Help the Living?

Three doctors from different countries discuss using the organs of dead people. Read the story and find out: Who is in favor of this? Who is opposed?

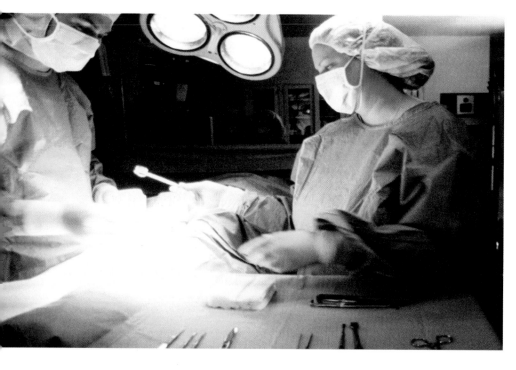

Dr. Jones: In my opinion, **the dead must help the living.** There is no question about it. When people die, they no longer have any use for their organs. If we don't use their healthy hearts or lungs, we miss the chance to save the lives of other people who need healthy organs.

In fact, it is so important to do this that I believe we must do it all of the time. **Every time there is a death, we should use all the organs we can, even if the person did not give permission before death.**

Dr. Tesfaye: I understand your position, Dr. Jones. But in my country, we have the opposite point of view. **We believe that it is wrong to cut up a dead body, take out the heart and then put it into someone else's body.**

Taking out parts of a dead person's body is a terrible thing to do. When you do that, you violate that person's body. When I die, I want my body to be treated with dignity and respect, and not cut open so that my organs can be put into other people.

Dr. Houte: As you two show, using organs from the dead to help the living is a difficult question. There are good reasons both to do it and not to do it. In my country, **we believe that it is all right to use organs from the dead but only under two conditions. First, the dead person must have given permission in writing, before he or she dies. Second, the person has to be dead.** Sometimes this is clear. But many times it is not. We all have heard stories of near-death experiences—when we think someone is dead, but he or she comes back to life.

And what about the so-called "brain-dead"? There are many people who are kept alive by machines—machines that breathe for them. But their brains are dead. What should we do with them? Turn off the machines and let them die so that we can use their healthy organs? I wonder if that isn't just the same as killing them. So we must be very careful before making any decisions.

IN THE GLOSSARY (PAGE 93)
• organs • lungs • give permission • violate • dignity • brain-dead

WHAT DO YOU THINK?

Which opinions do you agree with?
Check as many as you want.

❏ Well, organ donation is OK, but we have to be sure the person is dead! We have to make this clear before we can talk about donating organs.

❏ If people want to donate organs after they die, it's wonderful. But they should give permission before they die.

❏ I like the idea that the dead should help the living. I don't mind giving my organs if that helps people.

❏ Maybe it's OK to donate some organs, but not organs like the heart and the brain!

❏ I don't like the idea of cutting up my body after I die. I'm sorry, but I can't help you!

Now exchange your ideas with a classmate.

TURN TO PAGE 87 FOR AN INTERACTION TIP.

LOOKING AT THE ISSUE

What would you do to help someone stay alive?

Would you...	Yes, I'd do it	No, I wouldn't do it.
give blood?		
give a kidney to a dying family member?		
give your body to science after you die?		
register as a bone marrow donor?		
register as a donor at an eye bank?		
allow your doctor to transplant your organs after you die?		

Why or why not?

HOSTAGE

24

Ali has taken Flight 144 many times.
It was always long and boring. But this time,
something has happened. Read his story and find out:
What has happened on the flight?

I check my watch just after take-off and see that the flight is about 10 minutes behind schedule. That's nothing new, but the pilot always manages to land on time, in about five hours. So I close my eyes to rest a bit before the meal service.

Suddenly, loud shouts from the front of the plane startle me out of my nap. I hear more shouts, angry and threatening, and then a scream. I start to go forward to see what's wrong when a masked man waving a gun runs down the aisle, screaming at everyone to stay seated.

A hijack! The plane has been taken over by terrorists!

The terrorists are telling everyone to stay calm. **They say that nothing will happen to us if the pilot flies the plane to another country.** They say that they do not want to kill innocent people.

After three long, terrible hours, **the plane lands in the country where the terrorists want to go.** But then nothing happens. We sit in the hot plane for hours, waiting to be released.

The pilot announces that the terrorists have two demands. **First, the government must free some prisoners. Second, they want another plane so they can fly to a secret location.** At first, I am happy, thinking that we will all be free shortly. But the pilot says the government will not do that. **The terrorists have made a mistake and have landed in a country whose government refuses to talk to terrorists.** Its president says it will never yield to criminals and terrorists.

Our chances do not look good. There is no way that we can overpower the terrorists. They are heavily armed and watch us carefully. It is impossible to escape from the plane.

So here we sit, hostages in a life-or-death situation. The terrorists don't care about our lives. They are threatening to kill us, one by one. But the government says it will never talk to terrorists. They don't seem to care about our lives, either.

Will I get out of this situation alive?

IN THE GLOSSARY (PAGE 93)
• startle •threatening • a scream • a hijack • innocent
• prisoners • refuses • criminals • hostages

What do you think is the best thing to do?
Check the views you agree with.

❑ The government should never give in. If they give in to the terrorists, more hijackings will occur in the future.

❑ The plane should be allowed to fly to some other country whose government will talk to the terrorists.

❑ The government should talk to the terrorists. The passengers' lives are the most important thing.

❑ Another organization, like the United Nations, should talk to the terrorists.

❑ The police or army should secretly attack the plane and kill the terrorists.

Now exchange your ideas with a classmate.

*TURN TO PAGE 87 FOR AN **INTERACTION TIP.***

LOOKING AT THE ISSUE

In our society there are many kinds of threats. What should we do? For each case, decide what to do.

1. You are the president of a large company. A man phones you and threatens you. He says if you don't pay him $100,000 he will bomb the company building. What would you do?

   pay him   tell the police   ignore him   other:

2. You are in an elevator with a big man. He tells you to give him your money. He doesn't seem to have a gun or knife. What would you do?

   give him your money   try to get out of the elevator   ignore him   other:

3. You are the prime minister of your country. One of your ministers was kidnapped by terrorists. They say the government must free 10 people from prison or they will kill the minister. What would you do?

   free the prisoners   try to talk to the terrorists

   ignore them   other:

Do you know any other situations like these?

ISSUES IN SOCIETY

25

27

TO TELL OR NOT TO TELL

26

- Does society have a right to kill people?

- How should a murderer be punished?

- A mother explains her feelings about capital punishment.

A MOTHER'S STORY

WHY DON'T YOU ACCEPT US?

- Should everyone be treated with respect and fairness?

- Should homosexuals also be treated fairly?

- A man explains why he thinks he is not being treated fairly.

FINDERS KEEPERS

- What is an honest person?

- What should people do when they find something valuable?

- A man finds a lot of money and wonders what to do with it.

Helping OTHERS

Is helping strangers a good idea?
Read the story and find out:
What happened to this taxi driver when he tried to help?

A crazy man with three swords took over a city bus with 15 passengers and drove it wildly through the streets. But taxi driver Dal Chong Yang did not stop to think.

Driving his taxi as fast as possible, he caught up with the bus. He then drove in front of the bus for three kilometers, honking his horn and warning people to get out of the way. The bus hit his taxi five times, as the crazy man tried to kill Mr. Yang.

Finally, the bus hit a tree and came to a stop with all of its passengers safe. The crazy man was arrested by police.

Mr. Yang's action helped save many lives, police said. They believe that the crazy man wanted to run down as many people as he could with the bus.

The taxi driver, Mr. Yang, is now a hero. Everybody knows his name and praises his coura-

geous act. "I was afraid, of course," said Mr. Yang. "But I knew I had to do it or a lot of people would be hurt, maybe killed."

But some believe that what Mr. Yang did was wrong. "Ordinary people should not be trying to stop runaway buses and robberies," says the chief of police. "They really do not know how to do that, and they can get themselves injured or killed."

In fact, Mr. Yang was injured and nearly killed when the bus hit his car. He spent four months in the hospital and two months at home. Now he is back driving his taxi. But he can drive for only four or five hours each day because of the pain from his injuries, not like the 14 hours a day before his good deed.

WHAT DO YOU THINK?

Which opinions do you agree with?
Check as many as you want.

❏ I really believe we should help others —friends or strangers. If we don't, how cold and depressing this world would be!

❏ People should never help strangers for any reason. It's not a good idea.

❏ Ordinary people should not stop crimes. It's too dangerous.

❏ We should help others, but there's a limit to how much we should help.

❏ Why help others? We're all busy and have enough problems ourselves.

Now exchange your ideas with a classmate.

TURN TO PAGE 88 FOR AN INTERACTION TIP.

LOOKING AT THE ISSUE

Are you willing to help strangers? Read these situations and check your answers.

Case 1: You are walking down the street. A woman suddenly screams, "Help! A thief! Somebody get him!" and you see a man running away with the woman's purse. You decide to:

    run after the thief and try to catch him
    call the police
    scream, "Help! A thief!"
    ignore the whole thing and keep walking
    other:

Case 2: You are driving your car and see somebody on the roadside with a car problem. You decide to:

    stop and help, but only if it's a woman
    stop and help, but only if it's a woman or an old man
    stop and help, no matter who it is
    drive by without helping
    phone the police
    other:

A WOMAN'S PLACE

Professor Max Karlov has some controversial ideas about the role of women in society. Read this interview and find out: What message is Professor Karlov trying to give to the audience?

Interviewer: Congratulations, Professor Karlov, on your new book, *A Woman's Place.* I just finished reading it, and you really have strong ideas.

Professor Karlov: Yes. But my ideas are based on facts. **Societies all over the world are in trouble.** Now, you have to think, why are societies in trouble?

Interviewer: According to your book, Professor Karlov, you think **the difficulties in today's world are caused by a change in the natural order.** Could you explain that for our audience?

Professor Karlov: With pleasure. By a change in the natural order **I mean the changes in our society in the roles and responsibilities of men and women.** As everyone knows, what women do in society—their roles and responsibilities—has changed a great deal in the past 50 years.

Interviewer: OK, I think everyone would agree with that. But so what?

Professor Karlov: Women in many societies no longer stay at home and take care of children. They have jobs outside the home. This means they no longer have the time to take care of their children. In today's world, children grow up with so many problems. They drop out of school, they take drugs, they steal. Today's children are lazy and confused. They need the guidance, love and support that only mothers who are in the home can give. **Women should return to raising and educating children. They are naturally suited to do so. Men should continue to have the main responsibility for earning money for the family.** We know from history that men are suited for leadership and women are suited for raising children.

A woman's place is in the home, raising the children and keeping the home. A man's place is outside the home, working to support the family. I know this is an old-fashioned, or out-of-date, belief. But it is the one that fits the natural order.

IN THE GLOSSARY (PAGE 94)
• role • responsibilities • a great deal • guidance
• raising • educating • suited • an out-of-date belief

WHAT DO YOU THINK? What is your view of women's and men's roles?
Check the opinions you agree with.

❏ I think raising children and house-keeping should be done by both men and women.

❏ Men are naturally good at working outside the home and making money.

❏ If women stayed home, society would be much better.

❏ Women are naturally good at housekeeping and raising children.

❏ Today, to support a family, both the husband and wife need jobs.

Now exchange your ideas with a classmate.

TURN TO PAGE 88 FOR AN INTERACTION TIP.

LOOKING AT THE ISSUE Here are some of Professor Karlov's ideas.
For each of them, state an opposite or different idea.

Professor Karlov's Idea	Opposite Idea
Societies are in trouble because women have jobs outside the home.	Men have caused much of society's problems because most leaders are men.
Women are naturally suited to raising children.	
Men are natural leaders.	
A man's place is outside the home, working to support the family.	
Children need the help, love and support that only mothers who are in the home can give.	

To Tell or Not to Tell

Arafat, an employee of a large paper company, has made a shocking discovery. Read this letter to his brother and find out: What is happening at his company?

Dear Mohammed,

Thanks for the phone call yesterday; it was good to talk with you. You asked me if something was wrong, and I said no. But you were right, older brother—something is bothering me, troubling me greatly.

After talking to you yesterday, I decided to write you a letter. Writing often helps me organize my thoughts and see life more clearly. **I accidentally discovered that my company is dumping a chemical into a river near one of its factories in the countryside.** At first, I wasn't concerned about this. I knew that the owners of the company were fine men and would not do anything illegal.

But then I read a story in the newspaper about factories illegally dumping chemicals into rivers and how many of these chemicals are harmful. **One chemical is very dangerous to humans because, over time, it can cause cancer. And this is the same chemical that my own company is dumping into that river!**

I was puzzled at first. So I checked carefully and found out that I was right. **The company has been dumping this deadly chemical for about 18 months, and the owners know about it!**

Well, Mohammed, I am confused and upset. **Of course, I could tell my boss. But then he might tell the owners and they would fire me, the troublemaker.** Should I talk to officials of the government? The owners are powerful men and might bribe the officials, and then I would lose my job. Perhaps I could talk to the journalist who wrote the story in the newspaper.

As you know, **I plan to retire in four more years. I am too old to quit and find a new job. Besides, I like my work.** Well, I used to like my work. Now I am feeling very strange. It is getting difficult to continue my work as if nothing were wrong.

Please help me, older brother. I don't know what to do.

Yours,
Arafat

IN THE GLOSSARY (PAGE 94)
• an employee • accidentally • dump • a chemical • illegal
• puzzled • fire me • troublemaker • officials • retire

WHAT DO YOU THINK?

If you were Arafat's older brother, what would you tell him? Check the responses you agree with.

❏ Don't be afraid of losing your job. Be loyal to the community. Just think of the terrible danger to the people, especially the children, who play and fish in the river.

❏ Send unsigned letters to the people who live near the river and explain what's happening. Then they will start a protest.

❏ Don't say anything. Your job is too important. At your age, you'll never find another one.

❏ Talk to the journalist who wrote the story in the newspaper. Tell her everything. But make sure they keep your name secret.

❏ Keep your mouth shut. You should be loyal to your company.

Now exchange your ideas with a classmate.

TURN TO PAGE 88 FOR AN INTERACTION TIP.

LOOKING AT THE ISSUE

• Do you think it's cowardly to send an unsigned or anonymous letter?

    Yes   No   It depends

• In the following situations, would you give your name or remain anonymous? Why?

1. You have witnessed a car accident. Some people are seriously injured. You call the ambulance and the police.

    Give your name   Remain anonymous   Why:

2. You have witnessed a robbery in a store where you are shopping. You call the police.

    Give your name   Remain anonymous   Why:

3. You are writing a request card to a radio music program. Your name might be announced all over your country.

    Give your name   Remain anonymous   Why:

4. You donate a lot of money to charity. They want to list donors' names in the local newspaper.

    Give your name   Remain anonymous   Why:

Why Don't You Accept Us?

Wing and Jay have a special relationship that they must keep secret. Read the story and find out: Why can't they tell anyone?

Let me tell you about Wing. He's the funniest person I know—he can always make me laugh, even when I feel blue. He works hard at his job, and all his co-workers think he's great. He's interested in movies and tennis and politics, just like me. **He's the perfect partner—only I can't tell anyone.**

Wing and I are a couple —a homosexual, or gay, couple. We've been together for almost six years. That's a lot longer than some marriages last. We try to spend as much time together as we can, but because we are gay, there is always a problem.

When we go to parties, I can't introduce Wing as my partner. I have to say, "This is a friend of mine." We never go to the same restaurant more than once or twice together because people might notice us. We can't live together, as other couples do. No one wants to live near a homosexual couple.

I can't even tell my family about Wing. My parents don't know that I'm gay. They think there is something wrong with homosexuals, that we're not "normal." So my mother is always asking me, "When are you going to find a nice girl and get married?" I wish I could tell her that I've already found the right person for me. But my parents would never speak to me again. They would worry so much about what their friends would think of their homosexual son.

I know in some countries, like the United States, this is not such a big problem. But it is here.

I wonder why society isn't more understanding. **Why can't people accept us?** It's not fair. There is nothing wrong with Wing or with me. We are just like everyone else. We don't have a disease that other people might catch. We are normal, ordinary people who would like to be treated with respect.

Wing and I don't want any special treatment. We don't want to change the world. We just want to be together without hiding all the time. What's wrong with that?

IN THE GLOSSARY (PAGE 94)
• homosexual • gay • accept us • be treated with respect

Should people like Wing and Jay be able to live openly as a homosexual couple? Check your opinion.

❑ Sure. Gay people have the same right as everyone else to find a partner and be happy.

❑ I don't know. I just don't think society is ready to accept gays.

❑ I say no. It makes me really uncomfortable to be around people who are homosexuals.

❑ I say yes. If more gay couples lived openly, it would be easier for society to accept them.

❑ Absolutely not. Homosexuality is wrong.

Now exchange your ideas with a classmate.

TURN TO PAGE 89 FOR AN INTERACTION TIP.

LOOKING AT THE ISSUE

• What are some reasons for society to accept gay couples?

Homosexuals deserve to have partners and be happy.

• What are some reasons for society not to accept gay couples?

Many people think homosexuality is wrong.

Finder$ Keeper$

David always thought that he was
an honest person. But something happened
to him to make him wonder.
Read the story and find out: What happened?

Suddenly it was raining money. Money was falling from the sky and beginning to cover the ground like green snow.

David thought he was dreaming. He saw $100 bills everywhere. All he had to do was reach out and take a handful. He did. He did it again. And again. Soon he had more $100 bills than he could hold. **David saw an empty paper bag on the ground. He filled it up with more $100 bills.**

He looked up and saw, on the bridge over his head, an overturned truck. The truck had smashed into another truck. **The accident was so bad that all of the money the truck was carrying spilled into the road.** The wind was blowing hard, so the bills were floating all over.

David saw people running from everywhere. They were shouting to each other to hurry up. They were gathering money and putting it in purses and bags. He had never seen people working so quickly.

David then heard the sirens and saw the flashing lights on the police cars as they raced to the accident on the bridge. He left quickly.

When he got home, David counted the money he had picked up—almost $25,000. He had never seen so much money. And it was his! It belonged to him!

Or did it? David began to think about that. **Did it really belong to him? If it wasn't his, then whose money was it?** Well, thought David, it might belong to the bank. It was the bank's truck that crashed, and the money came from that truck.

But the money was just floating around. **He had not robbed a bank or stolen the money from somebody. What he had done was different. And nobody knew him.** Nobody could say that he had picked up the money. And then David thought of all of those other people who were picking up the money, just like he had done.

But David was worried. **He wondered if he should return the money.**

IN THE GLOSSARY (PAGE 94)
• an overturned truck • smashed into another truck • gathering money
• spilled into the road • floating around • robbed a bank

WHAT DO YOU THINK?

Should David keep the money or return it?
Check your opinion.

❏ He should keep it. I think the bank had insurance on the money, so nobody actually lost any money. So why not keep it?

❏ Of course he should return it. It's not his money. It's actually stealing, and stealing is wrong!

❏ He has to return it. Otherwise he will feel guilty.

❏ He should keep it. Nobody will know. He was lucky!

❏ Maybe he should return half of the money, just in case somebody saw him there.

Now exchange your ideas with a classmate.

Turn to Page 89 for an **INTERACTION TIP.**

LOOKING AT THE ISSUE

• If you found cash on the street, would you take it to the police? Or does it depend on the amount?

I would take the cash to the police if it were _____ or more, but I would keep it if it were less than that.

I would take it to the police whatever amount it was.

• What would you do in the following situations? Would you be honest? Or would you be "silent"?

	I'd be "silent."	I'd be honest.
Your paycheck is suddenly $1,000 more than usual.		
The clerk at a supermarket gives you change for a $100 bill, but it was actually a $50 bill.		
The waiter in a restaurant forgets to add $20 to your check for the bottle of wine you ordered.		
Your friend gives you $100 and says, "Thank you for lending me the money the other day." But you don't remember lending any money.		
One morning you find $1,000 cash in an envelope in your mailbox. Nothing is written on the envelope.		

A Mother's Story

*Have you ever
wished that another person
were dead?
This mother did.
Read the story and
find out:
Why did she want
a man to die?*

My heart jumped with joy when he was dead. I knew then, when the electricity was sent into that man's body, that I would finally have peace.

Am I a monster? Am I thirsty for blood? Do I get excited when people are killed? No, no, no! I am not a monster. **I am a mother whose 18-year-old son was killed during a robbery.**

Before Wang was killed, I had not thought much about capital punishment. Maybe I thought it was wrong. After all, killing someone who has killed someone else really doesn't help much. The other person is still dead, and killing the murderer just adds to the violence.

But that all changed when my only son was killed. **It happened five years ago. Wang was working at a grocery store.** He had just finished high school and was going to go to a good university in a month. He was working to earn money to help pay for his education.

Two men entered the store. They told my son to take all the money from the cash registers and put it in a bag. He did this. Then they ordered Wang to open the safe. Wang told them that he did not have the key. One of the men had a gun and threatened to shoot Wang. My son pleaded with him and told him that only the owner had the key. **The gunman then shot him five times** in the face and heart. **My son died instantly.**

Both robbers were captured. **The one who shot my son was sentenced to death in the electric chair. I asked to see him die.** I wanted to be there. I needed to be there. **My son's death had to be repaid.**

So I watched when they strapped him in. I saw him begging for his life. Good, I thought, beg all you can. You must die for what you did.

I think about capital punishment often now. **Killing is wrong. But if you kill, you should pay with your own life.** It's the only way we can stop all the violence.

IN THE GLOSSARY (PAGE 94)
• a monster • capital punishment • violence • cash registers
• safe • pleaded with him • instantly • were captured • repaid • strapped him in

WHAT DO YOU THINK?

Which opinions do you agree with?
Check as many as you want.

❏ If you kill someone, you have to die, too. That is your punishment. The only exception to capital punishment is self-defense.

❏ People who kill are crazy, insane. No one in his right mind would kill another person. That's why I think murderers should be put in mental hospitals.

❏ Capital punishment is wrong. We should never kill anyone, no matter how terrible the crime.

❏ Capital punishment is necessary. It helps prevent murder.

❏ Life in prison is the right sentence for a murderer.

Now exchange your ideas with a classmate.

TURN TO PAGE 89 FOR AN INTERACTION TIP.

LOOKING AT THE ISSUE

In which situations do you think it is OK to use the death penalty?

Criminal A kidnapped and killed a young child.

Criminal B set fire to a house, and the fire killed three people and injured many others.

Criminal C broke into a house, killed the two residents, and stole their money.

Criminal D went into a school yard and fired a machine gun, killing many schoolchildren.

Criminal E set a bomb to explode in an office building, killing many people.

Criminal F raped and killed several women.

Criminal G had her husband killed so that she would receive a large sum of insurance money.

The death penalty should never be used in any situation.

INTERACTION TIPS

1 "I think that…"

Use this phrase to give your opinion.

2 "What do you think?"

Use this question to ask for another person's opinion.

3 "I agree."

Use this expression when you agree with someone.

4 "Really? I think that…"

Use this expression when you do not agree with another person's opinion.

5 "I don't understand."

Use this expression when you don't understand what someone said.

6 "In my opinion…"

Use this phrase to give your opinion.

7 "What's your opinion?"

Use this question to ask for another person's idea.

8 "That's right."

Use this expression when you agree with someone.

9 "Well, I'm not sure."

Use this expression when you don't agree with someone's opinion.

10 "What do you mean?"

Use this question when you don't understand what someone said.

11 "Do you agree?"

Use this expression to ask for another person's opinion.

12 "So do I."

Use this phrase when you agree with someone.

13 "I'm afraid I disagree."

Use this expression when you don't agree with another person's opinion.

14 "What do you think about…?"

Use this expression to ask for another person's opinion.

15 "Could you repeat that?"

Ask this question when you don't understand what someone said.

16 "That's right. I agree with you."

Use this expression when you agree with someone.

17 "Really? I'm surprised you think that."

You can say this when you don't agree with another person's opinion.

18 "I don't understand. What do you mean?"

Try this when you don't understand what someone said.

19 "Do you agree? What do you think?"

This is another way to ask for a person's opinion.

20 "That's right! So do I!"

Use this expression when you agree strongly with another person.

21 "Well, I'm not sure. I'm afraid I disagree."

Use this expression when you do not agree with another person's opinion.

22 "What do you mean? Could you repeat that?"

You can say this when you don't understand what someone said.

23 "I agree completely."

Use this phrase when you really agree with someone.

24 "Really? I'm afraid I disagree."

Use this expression when you don't agree with another person's opinion.

25 "Could you say that again? I don't understand."

Use this expression when you don't understand what someone said.

26 "That's right! I agree with you completely."

Use this expression when you agree strongly with another person.

27 "Really? I'm afraid I disagree. I think that..."

Use this expression when you disagree with someone and you want to give your opinion.

28 "I agree with your point about..."

Use this phrase to show you agree with an idea that someone has.

29 "Yes, that's right. I agree with you about that."

Here's another expression to show you agree with someone.

30 "Well, I don't think so."

Use this expression when you don't agree with someone.

Here are some expressions to use when you exchange your opinions and ideas.

1 **"I think that…"**

Use this phrase to give your opinion.

For example:

"I think that it's a good idea to learn English."

Expressing Yourself

 "I think that learning English is a waste of time."

 "I think that it's a good idea to learn English."

2 **"What do you think?"**

Use this question to ask for another person's opinion.

For example:

"What do you think, Junko?"

Expressing Yourself

 "I think that marriage is giving up your freedom. What do you think, Junko?"

 "I think that marriage is a good idea."

3 **"I agree."**

Use this expression when you agree with someone.

For example:

"I agree with you."

Expressing Yourself

 "I think that eating meat is a good idea. What do you think, Junko?"

 "I agree with you."

80

4 "Really? I think that..."

Use this expression when you do not agree with another person's opinion.

For example:

> "I think our lifestyle is OK."
> "Really? I think that we need to change our lifestyle."

Expressing Yourself

 "I don't think the environment problems are very serious."

 "I agree."

 "Really? I think that we need to change our lifestyle."

5 "I don't understand."

Use this expression when you don't understand what someone said.

For example:

> "I don't understand, Richard."

Expressing Yourself

 "I think people shouldn't decide by money."

 "I don't understand, Richard."

6 "In my opinion..."

Use this phrase to give your opinion.

For example:

> "In my opinion, we should raise the price of gasoline."

Expressing Yourself

 "I think that we should develop solar cars."

 "In my opinion, we should raise the price of gasoline."

7 "What's your opinion?"

Use this question to ask for another person's idea.

For example:

> "What's your opinion, Ying-Che?"

Expressing Yourself

 "I think that abortion is wrong."

 "I agree. What's your opinion, Ying-Che?"

"In my opinion, abortion is OK, sometimes."

8 "That's right."

Use this expression when you agree with someone.

For example:

> "That's right, Mikyung."

Expressing Yourself

 "I think family harmony is important."

 "That's right, Mikyung. Family harmony *is* important."

9 "Well, I'm not sure."

Use this expression when you don't agree with someone's opinion.

For example:

> "Well, I'm not sure, Richard."

Expressing Yourself

 "Divorce is wrong. Husbands and wives should try to stay together."

 "Well, I'm not sure, Richard. When love ends, the marriage is over."

 "That's right, Junko."

10 "What do you mean?"

Use this question when you don't understand what someone said.

For example:

"What do you mean, Richard?"

Expressing Yourself

 "It's wrong to tell a lie."

 "What do you mean, Richard?"

 "We should always tell the truth."

11 "Do you agree?"

Use this expression to ask for another person's opinion.

For example:

"Do you agree, Junko?"

Expressing Yourself

 "Taking care of elderly parents is the child's duty. Do you agree, Junko?"

 "Well, I'm not sure."

 "What do you mean, Junko?"

 "When older parents live with their grown children, it causes problems."

12 "So do I."

Use this phrase when you agree with someone.

For example:

"So do I, Ying-Che."

Expressing Yourself

 "I think that giving money for working around the house is a bribe."

 "So do I, Ying-Che."

13 "I'm afraid I disagree."

Use this expression when you don't agree with another person's opinion.

For example:

"I'm afraid I disagree with you, Ying-Che."

Expressing Yourself

 "Men and women can be close friends without being lovers."

 "I'm afraid I disagree with you, Ying-Che."

 "What do you mean, Junko?"

"Men always want to have sex with women they like."

14 "What do you think about...?"

Use this expression to ask for another person's opinion.

For example:

"What do you think about pets and their owners, Junko?"

Expressing Yourself

 "What do you think about pets and their owners, Junko?"

 "I think that people treat their pets too much like humans."

 "Really? I think that people need pets for emotional support."

15 "Could you repeat that?"

Ask this question when you don't understand what someone said.

For example:

"Could you repeat that, Ying-Che?"

Expressing Yourself

 "Men and women from different countries should not get married."

 "Could you repeat that, Ying-Che?"

 "Yes. I think they shouldn't get married."

16 "That's right. I agree with you."

Use this expression when you agree with someone.

For example:

>"That's right, Richard. I agree with you."

Expressing Yourself

"I think if you kill someone in self-defense, you should not be punished."

"That's right, Richard. I agree with you."

"Well, I'm not sure."

"What do you mean, Ying-Che?"

"In my opinion, it's wrong to kill another person."

17 "Really? I'm surprised you think that."

You can say this when you don't agree with another person's opinion.

For example:

>"Really? I'm surprised you think that."

Expressing Yourself

"I think that money is the most important thing in the world."

"Really? I'm surprised you think that."

"Well, without money, people are unhappy."

"I'm afraid I disagree."

18 "I don't understand. What do you mean?"

Try this when you don't understand what someone said.

For example:

>"I don't understand, Mikyung. What do you mean?"

Expressing Yourself

"Best friends can trust each other."

"I don't understand, Mikyung. What do you mean?"

"They can tell each other their problems and secrets."

19 "Do you agree? What do you think?"

This is another way to ask for a person's opinion.

For example:

> "Do you agree, Junko? What do you think?"

Expressing Yourself

 "I'd like to know what is going to happen in the future. Do you agree, Junko? What do you think?"

 "I'm afraid I disagree, Richard."

 "What do you mean, Junko?"

"It's not a good idea to know the future. Life would be boring."

20 "That's right! So do I!"

Use this expression when you agree strongly with another person.

For example:

> "That's right, Richard. So do I!"

Expressing Yourself

 "I think that sick people should be told about their illness, even if they are dying."

 "That's right, Richard. So do I! Sick people have the right to know that."

21 "Well, I'm not sure. I'm afraid I disagree."

Use this expression when you do not agree with another person's opinion.

For example:

> "Well, I'm not sure. I'm afraid I disagree with you, Ying-Che."

Expressing Yourself

 "Doctors should never help people to die!"

 "Well, I'm not sure. I'm afraid I disagree with you, Ying-Che. I think doctors can help them avoid more suffering."

22 "What do you mean? Could you repeat that?"

You can say this when you don't understand what someone said.

For example:

> "What do you mean, Richard? Could you repeat that?"

Expressing Yourself

 "I think that near-death experiences aren't real."

 "What do you mean, Richard? Could you repeat that?"

 "In my opinion, these experiences can't really be true."

23 "I agree completely."

Use this phrase when you really agree with someone.

For example:

> "I agree completely, Mikyung."

Expressing Yourself

 "In my opinion, we should donate our organs after we die."

 "I agree completely, Mikyung."

 "Well, I'm not sure. I don't like the idea of donating my organs after I die."

24 "Really? I'm afraid I disagree."

Use this expression when you don't agree with another person's opinion.

For example:

> "Really? I'm afraid I disagree with you, Richard."

Expressing Yourself

 "The only way to stop terrorists is to kill them."

 "Really? I'm afraid I disagree with you, Richard."

25 "Could you say that again? I don't understand."

Use this expression when you don't understand what someone said.

For example:

"Could you say that again? I don't understand, Mikyung."

Expressing Yourself

 "We should help others, but it's up to us how much we should help."

 "Could you say that again? I don't understand, Mikyung."

"If you want to help someone, that's OK. But you don't have to help everyone all the time."

26 "That's right! I agree with you completely."

Use this expression when you agree strongly with another person.

For example:

"That's right! I agree with you completely, Junko."

Expressing Yourself

 "In my opinion, women should stay home and take care of children."

 "Really? I'm afraid I disagree with you, Mikyung. I think taking care of children and housekeeping should be done by both men and women."

 "That's right! I agree with you completely, Junko."

27 "Really? I'm afraid I disagree. I think that..."

Use this expression when you disagree with someone and you want to give your opinion.

For example:

"Really? I'm afraid I disagree. I think that employees should keep their mouths shut."

Expressing Yourself

 "I think employees should tell the newspaper if their company is doing something wrong."

 "Really? I'm afraid I disagree. I think that employees should keep their mouths shut."

28 **"I agree with your point about..."**

Use this phrase to show you agree with an idea that someone has.

For example:

"I agree with your point about families."

Expressing Yourself

 "I think that homosexuals have a difficult time in their families."

 "I agree with your point about families. I think the parents don't treat them fairly."

29 **"Yes, that's right. I agree with you about that."**

Here's another expression to show you agree with someone.

For example:

"Yes, that's right, Junko. I agree with you about that."

Expressing Yourself

 "When you find something valuable, you should keep it."

 "Yes, that's right, Junko. I agree with you about that. If you find it, it's yours."

30 **"Well, I don't think so."**

Use this expression when you don't agree with someone.

For example:

"Well, I don't think so, Richard."

Expressing Yourself

 "Capital punishment is wrong."

 "Well, I don't think so, Richard."

GLOSSARY

1 Why Learn English?

a waste of time - time used foolishly
to begin with - first
employees - company workers
literature - books, stories, poetry

2 Forever Single

attractive - good-looking
well-educated - studied at a good university
willingly - by your own choice
take each other for granted - stop thinking about how to make the other person happy
separated - apart from

3 What's for Dinner?

protein - a very important part of food
heart disease - a sickness that makes the heart very weak
destroys - kills
the environment - the earth and its forests, trees, rivers, lakes, air
export - send something from one country to another
cattle - cows

4 Last Chance

polluting the earth - making the earth very dirty and dangerous for people and animals
dump - throw away
warn - tell people about the dangers of something
population - people
scarce - not much of something
broke out - started
wealthy - rich

5 Take the Money and Run

contract - an agreement to do something or pay some money
owners - bosses
offer - promise to give something
earn - get
afford - be able to pay

6 Traffic Jam

traffic jams - too many cars and trucks
a flood of - very many, a great deal of
pollute - make very dirty and dangerous for people and animals
an exception - different from, not the same as
a permit - a license
a tax - an extra amount of money added to the cost of something

7 The Unborn Child

pregnant - expecting a child

fetus - the unborn baby

developing - growing

handicapped - having many problems or difficulties

mentally - in the mind or brain; mentally handicapped - problems which make a person unable to think well

physically - in the body; physically handicapped - problems with the body such as legs that don't work

depressed - very unhappy; sorrowful

abortion - ending a pregnancy before the baby is born

8 Family Harmony

simply - only

public school - school run by the government; usually the school is free

excellent - very, very good

crushed - very hurt

get over it - feel better after a period of time

9 For the Sake of the Children

depressed - very unhappy; sorrowful

stares at - looks very hard at

embarrassed - ashamed

get a divorce - end a marriage

for the sake of - because of

suffer - feel hurt or injured

bear - handle; take

10 Family Values

crash - the loud sound of an accident

upset - very worried

priceless - something so valuable it has no price

horrified - feeling shocked, terrible

looked guilty - looked as if he had done something wrong

worthless - having no value

precious - very, very valuable

11 Taking Care of Mother

forgetful - can't remember things easily

hire - give a job to someone

a housekeeper - someone who takes care of the house

pills - medicine

tiny - very small

commute - travel to work and back home

solution - the answer to a problem or a question

12 A Reward or a Bribe?

tasks - small jobs

trash - garbage

miss - forget to do something

a bribe - money you give to make sure someone does something

a reward - money you give to thank someone for doing something

13 Friends and Lovers?

shocked - very surprised

replies - answers

14 Tom Cat's Story

treats - deals with

lap - the top of a person's legs while seated

flea powder - medicine to kill small insects on cats and dogs

doesn't have a clue - has no idea

gourmet - very expensive

stinks - smells bad

managed to get out - escaped

chased - ran after

got me fixed - made me unable to father kittens

buried - put a dead body in the ground

15 An International Relationship

fit in - be a part of

miss - think about, want to be someplace or with someone

mixed marriages - marriages between people from different countries or cultures

confusing - making you feel unsure

16 20 Years of Pain

murdering - killing

kicked - hit with the foot

slapped - hit with an open hand, not a fist (closed hand)

choked - squeezed a person's neck or throat very, very hard

scars - old wounds or injury

stab - stick with a knife

right - what the law permits

punished - sent to jail or made to pay a fine for a crime

trial - a legal investigation to see if a person is guilty or innocent

in self-defense - hurting or killing a person who tried to hurt or kill you

17 Happily Ever After

over time - for a long period of time, such as five or 10 or 20 years

an accountant - a person who takes care of money

remain - continue

a promotion - a better job with the same company

refused - did not take

18 Growing Apart

graduate - finish high school or university

sharing our highs and our lows - telling each other when we are happy and sad

cut me off - quickly stopped my questions

behavior - way of acting with other people

hinted - made a suggestion very politely

19 Flight 77
weird - strange
ordinary - not special or different
passengers - people who are traveling on a plane, boat or bus
crash - run into, hit against something, and break apart

20 Doing the Right Thing
cancer - a serious illness in which sick body cells increase
an operation - cutting open a body in order to take out or repair the bad part
heartbroken - very sad and upset
an ulcer - a sore area inside your stomach, which sometimes bleeds
disease - illness
be informed - be told about
shorten - make something shorter
persuade - cause someone to do something by giving a good reason for doing it

21 The Right to Die
a deadly mixture of drugs - a number of medicines mixed together that can kill a person
nerve cells - cells that send and receive messages between the brain and other parts of the body
spinal cord - many nerves together inside your spine that connect your brain to nerves in all parts of your body
paralyzing - making your body or part of your body unable to move
gradually - little by little
a coffin - a box in which a dead person is buried
become a vegetable - become very sick and be unable to move or do anything or enjoy anything
regardless of - even if

22 Alive or Dead?
recovering - getting better
floating - up in the air
weightless - having no weight, very light
a sensation - a feeling
wail - a long, loud sound like crying
an ambulance - a car that carries sick or injured people to a hospital
shrugged his shoulders - raised his shoulders to show he didn't know what to do
given up - stopped trying
emotion - feelings
a smashed body - a broken body

23 Should the Dead Help the Living?
organs - parts of your body
lungs - body parts inside your chest which you use for breathing
give permission - say OK to do something
violate - treat badly
dignity - true worth and respect
brain-dead - the heart is still beating but the brain is not working any more

24 Hostage
startle - surprise and frighten
threatening - frightening
a scream - a loud cry or shout
a hijack - taking control of a plane by force while it is flying from one place to another
innocent - simple, harmless
prisoners - people kept in a prison for some crime
refuses - says "no" to
criminals - people who commit (do) a crime
hostages- people who are caught by a person or group and who may be killed

25 Helping Others
honking - making a short loud sound with a car horn
warning - telling about a dangerous problem
get out of the way - escape
was arrested - was caught by the police
praises - speaks highly of somebody or something
courageous act - a difficult or dangerous act
injured - hurt
good deed - an action that helps others

26 A Woman's Place
role - their position, what they are expected to do
responsibilities - duties
a great deal - very much
guidance - help and advice
raising - bringing up
educating - teaching
suited - fit for
an out-of-date belief - an idea that people believed a long time ago, but not now

27 To Tell Or Not To Tell
an employee - a company worker
accidentally - by chance
dump - throw away
a chemical - something that is made by a chemical process, something not natural
illegal - against the law
puzzled - confused
fire me - take away my job
troublemaker - someone who causes trouble
officials - people in high positions in an organization
retire - leave the job and stop working

28 Why Don't You Accept Us?
homosexual - a person who is attracted to people of the same sex
gay - homosexual
accept us - allow us to live the way we want to
be treated with respect - be talked to politely and allowed to do what other people do

29 Finders Keepers
an overturned truck - a truck on its side or upside down
smashed into another truck - hit against another truck and broke
gathering money - picking up money
spilled into the road - came out from the truck and went into the road
floating around - moving slowly through the air
robbed a bank - stole money from a bank

30 A Mother's Story
a monster - a very bad person
capital punishment - punishing somebody by death
violence - using force to hurt or harm
cash registers - business machines used in stores to calculate and record money
safe - a strong metal box with a lock to keep money or important things
pleaded with him - begged, asked him from the heart
instantly - at once
were captured - were caught
repaid - paid back
strapped him in - tied him into the electric chair

OTES

NOTES